1111 Magical Affirmations

Empowering Your Mind For Ultimate Manifestation

1111 Magical Affirmations

EMPOWERING YOUR MIND FOR ULTIMATE MANIFESTATION

ROBERT ZINK
With AGNE LECOCQ

1111 Magical Affirmations

Empowering Your Mind For Ultimate Manifestation

By Robert Zink
With Agne Lecocq

Law of Attraction Solutions, LLC
2023

Copyright © 2023 by Robert Zink & Rachael Zink

All rights reserved. No part of this book, including text, images, and tables may be reproduced or utilized in any form or by any information storage and retrieval system, without permission in writing from the authors and publisher.

The phrases found in this book which are all registered trademarks include but are not limited to the following: Miracle Mentoring and Alchemy Success Coaching, Miracle Mentoring, Miracle Hypnosis, and Neurolinguistic Alchemy

Cover Design By Tressa Whitman

First Edition: 2023
ISBN 978-0-9908250-7-4

Published by

Law of Attraction Solutions, LLC
34522 N Scottsdale Rd
Scottsdale, AZ 85266

www.LawOfAttractionSolutions.com

*Dedicated to
all those individuals
that have made
spreading the message
of personal empowerment possible
through clear intentions
and affirmations.*

Forward

Table of Contents

Forward ....- 11 -
Introduction ....- 16 -
   What Is An Affirmation?..- 16 -
   How Do Affirmations Work? ....- 18 -
   How To Reprogram Your Subconscious Mind And Why It Is Important ....- 20 -
   Always Use Present Tense ....- 21 -
   Affirmation Should ALWAYS Be Followed By A Positive Statement. ....- 22 -
   Emotionalize Your Affirmations ....- 23 -
   How, When, And For How Long Should You Practice Your Affirmations? ....- 24 -
   Seven Powerful Ways To Practice Your Affirmations..- 26 -
   The Law Of Assumption And The Use Of "I AM" Affirmations ....- 35 -
Miracles..- 40 -
   MIRACLES ....- 41 -
Personal Empowerment ....- 47 -
   CONFIDENCE ....- 48 -
   SELF-LOVE..- 54 -
   RAISING YOUR VIBRATION ....- 58 -
   OVERCOMING BLOCKAGES ....- 61 -
   SELF-EMPOWERMENT...- 63 -
   LIFE PURPOSE ....- 65 -
Love & Relationships ....- 67 -
   HEALING YOUR ROMANTIC RELATIONSHIP OR MARRIAGE ....- 68 -
   ATTRACTING YOUR SOULMATE ....- 75 -
   ATTRACTING YOUR PERFECT RELATIONSHIP OR MARRIAGE..................................- 79 -
   MANIFESTING PREGNANCY..- 86 -
   GETTING OVER A BREAK-UP..- 91 -
   HEALING YOUR RELATIONSHIP WITH A FAMILY MEMBER, FRIEND, OR COLLEAGUE ....- 93 -
Money & Wealth ....- 96 -
   MANIFESTING MONEY ....- 97 -
   WINNING LOTTERY...- 103 -
Business & Career ....- 107 -

- HEALING YOUR BUSINESS .... - 108 -
- MANIFESTING YOUR OWN BUSINESS .... - 111 -
- JOB/CAREER .... - 114 -

Success & Abundance .... - 118 -
- ATTRACTING SUCCESS .... - 119 -
- TO STOP PROCRASTINATING .... - 122 -
- ABUNDANCE AND PROSPERITY .... - 125 -

Health & Wellbeing .... - 128 -
- MANIFESTING PERFECT HEALTH .... - 129 -
- PERFECT BODY WEIGHT .... - 132 -
- REVERSING AGING .... - 137 -

Healing & Clearing .... - 140 -
- HEALING BETRAYAL .... - 141 -
- HEAL ANXIETY .... - 145 -
- HEAL DEPRESSION .... - 148 -
- HEAL ABANDONMENT .... - 151 -

Source Connection .... - 154 -
- LAW OF ATTRACTION .... - 155 -
- THE UNIVERSE .... - 158 -
- MORNING AFFIRMATIONS .... - 160 -
- SPIRITUAL .... - 163 -

Children .... - 165 -
- AFFIRMATIONS FOR CHILDREN .... - 166 -

Gratitude .... - 168 -
- GRATITUDE .... - 169 -

SUMMARY .... - 174 -

A S K F I R M A T I O N S .... - 177 -
- NOTES .... - 181 -
- NOTES .... - 182 -

Forward

Written by
Miracle Mentor & Alchemy Success Coach
Agne Lecocq

I met Robert Zink during one of the darkest moments in my life. I will spare you the details, but I really felt that my world fell apart. I felt lost, I felt broken, I felt unworthy, I felt scared of the unknown. I was in physical and mental pain. Most importantly, I felt unfulfilled, I had no direction in my life, and I no longer knew who I was and why I was here. **I AM** Agne Lecocq, and I would like to share how I have transformed my life, so that you too can do the same. When I met Robert, I was aware of The Law of Attraction, and I used it to manifest some great things. However, it was RANDOM, it was not CONSISTENT, it was not INTENTIONAL enough. I did not fully embody it. It was something that I DID every now and then, but it was not part of my identity. It was not part of my life. I did not live my life as a conscious co-creator. I did not live my life as a conscious manifestor.

In my mid-thirties, my life fell, and I faced an identity crisis. When I met Robert Zink, my true journey of "**I AM**" and becoming a co-creator started. In his book

"Law of Attraction Secrets," Robert writes, "Forget about finding yourself! You are not lost, so there is no need to discover or find yourself. You are simply what you choose to create. GO create yourself! BE who you desire to become." These lines really hit home, and they will be stuck with me forever. I realized it is not the question "Who am I?" but instead, "Who do I decide to become? Who do I desire to be? Who do I CHOOSE to be!". That was a game-changer for my entire life. I went from being a victim to being a victor. My mindset went from believing that my life is happening to me to believing that my life is happening through me. I began actively co-creating my reality through the thoughts that I think, the words that I speak, the feelings that I feel, the beliefs that I hold, and the actions I take. All these elements are relevant, yet it all starts with beliefs.

Robert has taught me how important our beliefs are. They play a crucial role in shaping our lives. Therefore, it is important to work with them. Sooner or later, we will see their physical manifestation in our reality. In terms of manifestation, energy always becomes matter.

Many beliefs are the results of what we affirm to ourselves daily. Our mind learns through repetition. We think around 60 to 80 thousand thoughts per day. A belief is nothing but a thought that has been repeated over and over again. Therefore, you can choose your beliefs and reprogram the existing ones. You can heal your subconscious mind and your life with the help of the right affirmations. You can "program" yourself for success, everlasting friendships, incredible relationships, epic experiences, a business that flourishes, an adventurous and fulfilling life, and living your life to your fullest potential. Yes, it is that powerful!

One of the first things I teach people I empower is that manifesting is becoming. To manifest your desires, you must go through a rebirth process. Everything that is present in your life today is not random. You have created it. So, if the old you did not give you the world you wanted, then you will have to create a new you. You cannot manifest a new world operating from your old consciousness.

The most important question you need to ask yourself is "what do I need to become in order to manifest what I desire?" Do I need to work on my limiting beliefs? Do I need to work on controlling my emotions or letting go of my past? Am I keeping myself trapped in the old emotions and pain, unable to move forward? Do I need to become more confident? Do I need to fill my cup of self-love? Do I need to become more graceful and compassionate? No matter what the question is, it all starts with two short, simple, powerful, and yet most potent words, "**I AM**."

Affirmations are one of the most incredible tools of manifestation. Affirmations are about the becoming and transformation that you desire to see in your life. Robert has taught me many ways to use and create affirmations so that I can activate their limitless power to transform my life. Affirmations will invoke the energy that the Universe uses to create miracles.

"**I AM**" will help you make your desired manifestation part of your reality right now. These two powerful words will bridge the gap between where you are and where you desire to be. We can never manifest something that we are separate from because that creates a vibrational mismatch in energies. Lack and need cannot manifest abundance. We always manifest what we are, not what we want. **I AM** is the present, it is the now, so whatever you are asking or invoking into your life, you are being it NOW.

I believe affirmations are one of the best known and widely used tools of manifestation, yet also the most misunderstood. Two things are crucial to effective affirmations. The first is you need to activate your affirmations by emotionalizing them. The second is the need to follow your affirmations with an action, either inspired or aligned action.

If you repeat your affirmations like a parrot that does not understand what it says, you will get the same results as doing nothing at all. Strictly repeating affirmations will not activate them in your subconscious to shift your reality. Thanks to Robert, I discovered the true magic of the affirmations and learned how to activate them in my reality.

Forward

Today, I understand that every affirmation is a seed you plant into your subconscious mind. When you continue nurturing that seed with attention, intention, care, and love, the seed will sprout and start taking root in your conscious and subconscious mind. This will incite the process of transformation and becoming your new reality. It will start slowly changing your thoughts, beliefs, and feelings.

Every morning when I wake up, I choose how I want to show up in the world. Today is always the day I choose who I desire to be. My creations are no longer random or unconscious. I have created a purposeful, happy, and abundant life. **I AM** is your prayer that will connect you to the Source of the Universe. "**I AM**" allows the Source to pour blessings into your life. The Source of the Universe gives because you asked. The Source of the Universe gives because you believed. The Source of the Universe gives because you affirmed. You will live in a new reality because in your thoughts, mind, actions, and energy field you *became* that which you desired to attract. You will manifest your deepest desires and your wildest dreams!

Agne Lecocq

Miracle Mentor & Alchemy Success Coach

Introduction

What Is An Affirmation?

I AM divine. **I AM** abundant. **I AM** limitless. **I AM** beautiful and courageous. **I AM** enough. **I AM** healthy. **I AM** happy. **I AM** capable of doing great things. **I AM** successful in every area of my life. **I AM** able to achieve great things in my life. **I AM** wealthy. **I AM** harmonious. **I AM** at peace.

Money is easy to make. Every day in every way, my life is getting better and better. My life is a gift. I choose to see all the opportunities surrounding me. Everything that I need comes to me at the right moment. I trust myself to create an amazing life. The one I desire also desires me. Miracles are part of my life.

An affirmation is a statement about yourself, your abilities, your environment, your relationships, or any area of your life that you either consciously or unconsciously repeat to yourself. Affirmations can be positive and inspiring or negative. Remember, the Law of Attraction is impartial, so you always manifest what you focus on and what you believe to be true.

Introduction

There are no two words more powerful when it comes to attracting and manifesting affirmations than the words "**I AM**". The statement "**I AM**" is the most potent statement one can ever think, write or speak. If you monitor your thoughts closely, you will be shocked at all the "**I AM**" affirmations you say daily. "**I AM** tired. **I AM** going to be late for work. **I AM** looking good today," and so on. You are so good at making **I AM** affirmations that you did it subconsciously. What you believe about who you ARE will determines the speed of your manifesting. Manifesting is attracting things, people, and experiences from the infinite field of potential to your physical world. You can only achieve that when you are one with your desire in your conscious and subconscious. You can expect your miracle if your vibration and energy matches your desires When you emotionalize the feelings you will have when your desire is manifested, you can expect it even faster. So, who will you create yourself to be with "**I AM**" affirmations? Who are you, and what are you?

I invite you to reflect on the things that you are affirming to yourself on a daily basis. Every "**I AM**" statement is a seed you plant in your mind and energy field. Every "**I AM**" is a manifestation that will take place despite its energy connotations, which may be positive or negative. It has been estimated by experts that a person thinks around 50,000 to 70,000 thoughts per day. Around 80% of them being the same as the day before and negative. Are you aware of the affirmations you choose to listen to on repeat daily?

Every time you start your sentence with the words **"I AM,"** whether knowingly or not, you address your subconscious mind. You are imprinting your subconscious mind with the vibration of what you manifest. Once burned in your subconscious mind auto manifestation kicks off.

How Do Affirmations Work?

Affirmations work through matriculation. Little by little, they begin to matriculate into the subconscious mind. Over a period of days and weeks, sometimes months, you can shift your inner dialog. It all depends on how much conscious action you take. It may take a long time, if you have a lot of resistance to controlling your mind. Therefore, if you have done your affirmations for a couple of weeks or a month, but you see no changes, it's not a reason to give up but a reason to continue with even more conscious awareness and belief.

When you use your affirmations consistently, it imprints into your subconscious mind. In the beginning, when you start practicing your new affirmations and your new

Introduction

state of being, it might feel like a lie. It may feel uncomfortable, weird, or it might bring up your buried pain, trauma, and wounds. The key is to continue doing your affirmations until you can feel the outcome you desire.

Your subconscious mind does not have eyes, so it starts believing whatever you tell it. It does not know the difference between what is real and what you imagine. Therefore, if you persist in your desire, it slowly starts to believe it as the truth. You become what you believe, and you believe what you affirm. A thought, a statement, an affirmation that you repeat over and over again becomes your belief. It becomes a part of your programming.

An example is when you, as an adult, free to make any choice you want, hear the voice of a parent telling you to do it differently. These affirmations are used so often they become beliefs in your reality.

You came to this world as pure light and love. When growing up, your environment, conditioning, and ego made you believe you are less. You forgot about the Divine Spark in you. Yet, you still have an Infinite Life Force within you. You still are an extended part of the Divine Source Energy. So if the Divine or the Universe is not limited to anything, and you are an extension of it, then you are not limited to anything, either!

Your manifesting powers, vibrations, and energy are directly related to what you believe about yourselves. **I AM** affirmations will bring you back to the center of Divine Power, to the blissful state where you know you are enough just as you are. You live in a state where you are beautiful, loved, and appreciated just because you ARE. Affirmations will help you reconnect to your divine spark and highest potential. Therefore, you will create the most beautiful and fulfilling life you desire; the life you are meant to live.

How To Reprogram Your Subconscious Mind And Why It Is Important

Around 95% of human behavior comes from the subconscious mind. So, you are not really manifesting with your conscious mind but your subconscious mind. Your subconscious mind is where your fears, traumas, doubts, behavior patterns, and beliefs live. Your beliefs create your reality; you can never create the life you desire and deserve if you hold onto your limiting beliefs. The wrong beliefs will stop your manifestations and make you attract the exact opposite of what you desire.

With the help of "**I AM**" affirmations, you can reprogram your mind, replace your limiting beliefs, and manifest the life of your dreams. Create a new **I AM** identity, therefore a new life. Repetition and consistency are relevant, and so is the effort to really charge all your affirmations emotionally. When you truly start believing all the empowering things about yourself, you can sit back and watch your life blossom and see all your desires show up in your reality.

Always Use Present Tense

All the energy of creation is always in the now. Therefore, **I AM**/other affirmations are always used in the present tense. It is who you are being right now. The "**I AM**" affirmations will help you raise your vibration to a higher consciousness and help you to transform your energy field through releasing incredible, almost unstoppable energy.

You have to become one with your desire. You have to embody it. When you say "**I AM**" in the present tense, you become one with your desire. You connect to that potential, to its frequency, to its vibration. You become it, and it becomes you. When you become one, there is no longer any separation between you and your desire; that is when the Law of Attraction works to its fullest power. That's when instant manifestations take place.

Affirmation Should ALWAYS Be Followed By A Positive Statement.

The words "**I AM**" hold a mighty force of creation, and the words that follow them are summoning a manifestation because you declare it to be a fact. You are declaring it to be true. You impress your conscious and, most importantly, your subconscious mind with this belief.

You only want to use positive statements. For example, change "**I AM** not late" to "**I AM** on time". In the same way, change "**I AM** not sick" to "**I AM** healthy; **I AM** healing." When it comes to love change "**I AM** not single" to "**I AM** in a loving and fulfilled relationship". If you seek financial freedom, change "I no longer have to worry about money" to "**I AM** financially abundant." It is because your mind always picks the keywords in a phrase, so it hears - late, sick, single, worry. Start forming your affirmations so your mind hears positive words.

It goes without saying, that all the other negative statements and affirmations like "I always make stupid mistakes, **I AM** too old to change careers, **I AM** not smart enough, **I AM** going to stay single all my life, nobody loves me, my partner will cheat on me, they will never hire me for that job, I cannot find a solution to this problem" will program your subconscious and will become self-fulfilling prophecies.

I kindly invite you to use the two most powerful words "**I AM**" to your advantage: **I AM** happy. **I AM** healthy. **I AM** in love. **I AM** loved. **I AM** amazing. **I AM** called to this Earth to create beautiful things. **I AM** here to leave a legacy.

Emotionalize Your Affirmations

Neville Goddard said, "Feeling is the Secret," and I couldn't agree more with him. Affirmations do not work unless they are emotionalized. Emotions and feelings ACTIVATE your affirmations. They bring it to life and invoke the frequency and vibration of the desires and statements that you affirm.

When you start feeling an emotion, and you hold it for a little while, you start vibrating it. It becomes part of your energy field, and the longer you hold it, the stronger its presence in your vibration. You must see and FEEL what it is like to be happy and rich, be in that loving relationship, drive that car of your dreams, take that dream vacation, buy that dream home, or meet your soulmate. You need to put some energy into this. What does it feel like? What does it smell like? What does it look like? What does it sound like? What does your body feel?

How, When, And For How Long Should You Practice Your Affirmations?

    You can practice your affirmations in so many different ways. You can say them out loud or in your head. You can listen to them, or you can read them. You can make a mind movie. You can make a vision board that has images AND affirmations on it. You can record your own affirmations and listen to them either in your waking state or while sleeping. Hearing your own voice can be very powerful because when you sleep, your conscious and analytical minds are not active, and everything goes straight into your subconscious mind. You can also listen to subliminal meditations recorded by Law of Attraction experts such as the meditations on MiracleHypnosisOnline.com.

    You can also write your affirmations with physical paper and pen. This is a very powerful practice to connect your imagination with the reality you desire to manifest.

Introduction

When you write down your dreams, goals, and affirmations, something magical happens. A writing technique called "scripting" invokes tactile energy. There is something about taking the idea, thought, or affirmation and bringing it down through your nervous system through the muscles and onto the page in written form. Your subconscious mind takes note. It is also imprinted by or through the image of your dream written down. Your dreams, aspirations, and visions live in the spiritual world, in the energetic world, so when you write them down, you bring them into this physical world, so you actually connect the two worlds.

Physical memorization will imprint your affirmations even deeper into the quantum manifesting field. You should always know your affirmations by heart. It's ok to read them for the first few times initially, but you want to memorize them as soon as possible. Your affirmations are your new identity and part of who you are. So, in the same way you would not falter when somebody asks for your name, create the same certainty and familiarity with your affirmations.

The best time to do your affirmations is right after you wake up or just before you fall asleep. These are two powerful times, two windows in a day when your mind is in that twilight zone. This is where you are neither asleep nor awake, and the access to your subconscious mind is wide open. For listening to subliminal audios with affirmations, the night is the most powerful moment because everything goes straight into your subconscious mind.

How long should you say an affirmation? If you have a specific goal, or specific dream to manifest, you can stop your affirmations when you attract it. For other affirmations, revisit, upgrade, update, and continue practicing! I have affirmations I have been practicing for years and don't plan to ever stop them. These affirmations are the keys to your energy field and personal values.

Seven Powerful Ways To Practice Your Affirmations

1. Choose a couple of affirmations that seem most relevant for your life right now; print or write them, frame them, and put them in places you see regularly, in your home and at your work. Get beautiful frames, choose fancy fonts, and go for big letters. It will capture your subconscious mind's attention whether you are aware of it or not. Around 75% of all the sensory information that your brain processes comes in through your sight.

Introduction

Your subconscious mind constantly observes your environment and is processes experiences that it hears, sees, and perceives. Remember, it is your subconscious mind that you are seeking to imprint! So, as you will be going through your day, and even if you might not pause to deliberately read and state the affirmation, your subconscious mind will capture it every time you pass them.

Repetition and consistency are essential because that is how your subconscious mind learns and assimilates things. Not only that, but it will also conjure a beautiful feeling that you will keep tuning into. Images and feelings are a powerful combination to rewrite your subconscious programming. Framed affirmations, therefore, are an incredible way to plant a seed in your subconscious mind.

It is important to surround yourself with empowering symbols. Affirmations are symbols. These symbols invoke a feel-good emotion, positive energy, and the inherent energy of the things you desire to manifest in your life. An environment that is full of symbols is an environment that supports your goals and helps you to reach the success you desire, whatever that may be. The symbols in a church, school, or a rock concert are all very different. Those symbols create different energy for different types of manifestation.

2. Create beautiful affirmation cards that you can take with you. Choose a size that is convenient for you: it can be bigger, or it can be smaller. Choose paper, motifs, and colors that will enforce the energy of your affirmations. Write one affirmation per card. Make as many cards as you wish. And take them with you wherever you go.

As you go about your day, use them whenever you are inspired to do so. You can make affirmation cards for every area of your life – love, relationships with others, work, health, financial abundance, your business, ideas, opportunities.

Your vibration will be different every day. Each day you can either make your own if you like. You can select a different topic for each day or just recite all of the ones you feel aligned with. Most importantly, always emotionalize your affirmations because your emotion and energy "activate" your affirmations.

3. Use affirmations on your vision board. Your affirmations carry a very strong energy and enormous potential of your manifestation. They are not mere words; they are your intentions. Affirmations carry your personal power and creative energy. Traditional vision boards only contain images. You can also use an affirmation with each image to increase its power. "**I AM**" affirmations are the most powerful. The following are just a few examples. "**I AM** manifesting money from unexpected sources." "**I AM** enjoying my amazing vacation in Maldives." "**I AM** a happy owner

Introduction

of a new beautiful home." "**I AM** pregnant." "**I AM** a career magnet." "**I AM** attracting excellent job prospects all the time."

When you use affirmations on a vision board, you are connecting the two worlds; the physical and the spiritual. The spiritual world is the invisible realm where your dreams are born, and then there is this physical world where you see them manifest in a physical form. With regular use of the vison board, the images will immediately invoke your affirmations. Every affirmation denotes that **I AM** is a state. When you put an image of your dream house and connect it with the affirmation "**I AM** a happy owner of my new beautiful home," that affirmation helps you to shift from the state of wanting to the state of being. **I AM** one with my desire. **I AM** my desire. That is the most magnetic power and energy that no wish or desire can resist.

4. Say, whisper, or repeat your affirmations in your head just before falling asleep. That little window between your waking state and sleep that occurs just before you fall asleep is a very powerful time to burn your affirmations into your subconscious mind. In your waking state, your analytical mind runs the show and stands guard to the realm of your subconscious mind. That is why it will bounce off any affirmation not complying with your current reality. For example if you have debts, and you are using affirmations like, "**I AM** financially independent," "I have

more than enough money," or "My life is abundant," your brain, and your conscious mind hearing that will go "Hell NO!" Your consciousness will generate counter intentions, counter thoughts, and even more fears. The conscious mind is all about logic and that which you are trying to assert is not logical at all; it is a lie to your conscious mind.

However, just before falling asleep, you get into a state where you are easily suggestible because the activity of your brainwaves slows down, and you start slipping into what is called Theta brainwaves. You are now standing on the threshold between your waking state and sleep. The analytical and conscious minds are no longer present, and you have a wide access to your subconscious mind. Your subconscious mind is like a four-year-old; it believes everything you say to it. The subconscious cannot and will not analyze, compare or try to assess what is true and valid or what is possible and what is not possible. It will accept and allow everything that you say to it. As you sleep, the subconscious will communicate with the conscious mind to seek expression in the outer world, in the reality you desire.

Since there are some programs and beliefs in your subconscious mind already, it is not enough to do it once. Reprogramming takes time. Your subconscious mind learns through repetition. Be consistent in your effort. Moreover, your subconscious mind never sleeps, so if you fall asleep with specific affirmations or thoughts, your subconscious mind will continue working on assimilating that information while you sleep.

5. Drink your affirmations. Yes, you read it right. Speak your affirmations into a glass of water and then drink it. You will manifest from the inside out because every cell in your body will now be infused with the energy and intention of your affirmation. Water is alive. Water has consciousness, and it can take on your intention. A Japanese scientist and researcher, Dr. Masaru Emoto, spent his whole life studying how water and its molecules can be affected by your thoughts, intentions, and words. He conducted extensive experiments with his team that proved that water responds to energies and vibrations that it was exposed to. The water itself has a neutral vibration and acts therefore, as a conduit to human thoughts, energy, and words. Deliberate human interaction physically alters the molecular structure of water. Love, gratitude, compassion, joy, and all the other high vibrational emotions create beautiful snowflake-like patterns in water. So take a glass of freshly poured water, hold it with your hands, and whisper all your amazing affirmations and desires that you want to infuse into your water. You can say things like, "**I AM** waking up to an amazing day," "Today my life will be filled with amazing opportunities," "Blessings are pouring into my life today and every day," "Today **I AM** the most confident loving and productive

version of myself," "**I AM** proud of myself," "**I AM** loved," "**I AM** enough," "**I AM** creating the life of my dreams," or "**I AM** blessed with miracles." Allow your voice and its vibration to touch the surface of the water gently. After you feel you have infused your water, drink it. Visualize how your intention and your affirmation are infused into your whole body.

6. Take your affirmations to your shower. Life can get busy, and it often does. Therefore, carving out time during your day for different manifestations can be challenging. Prioritize affirmations as part of your daily routine is always a good idea. This way, you will always be sure to do them, and it will become a habit. And as John Dryden said, "First we make our habits, then our habits make us." Make no mistake, practicing your affirmations is a very powerful habit that will transform you. So why affirmations in the shower? A shower is something that you do every day, and it is a place where you naturally feel more relaxed. Showers open your energy field making you more suggestable to new ideas. Taking a shower does not require your undivided attention or concentration.

Laminate an A4 or any other format page with affirmations for all the areas of your life, and you are ready. Read, repeat, and emotionalize them as you shower daily. Again, because you are relaxed, you might find yourself drifting away or getting carried away by one of the affirmations every now and then, but that is ok. Pick it up where you left off when you catch yourself off track.

Besides the convenience, here are two other reasons why affirmations in a shower are a good idea. Water has the power to cleanse and purify, so every time you shower, you purify your energies. When you are clean and clear, you make room to move into the state of receiving. Secondly, if you shower in the morning, not only will you be working towards a specific goal or dream, but you will be setting a powerful intention for your day and infusing it with the beautiful energies of your being.

7. Create a sigil from your affirmation. This is an extraordinary method and a special way to use your affirmations. It is incredibly powerful because one more time, you will not be working with your conscious mind but your subconscious mind. Step number one is choosing or creating clear, powerful, capturing affirmations. Step number two is creating a sigil. If you haven't heard about a sigil, it is a symbol or an image that you create and use to bring your desire to manifest through the power of your subconscious mind. There is more than one way of doing it. Do a little research and see what speaks to you. Most important is not to focus too much on the aesthetics but allow your intuition to guide you.

Step number 3 is to charge your sigil. You need to attach your wish, desire and new reality to it. A sigil can be charged through emotional, spiritual, or sexual energy. You may not always have time for lengthy meditations or rituals, but you can attach and anchor their energy to a symbol. Your unique sigil will awaken manifestation energy every time you see it. Just like Macgregor Mathers expressed, "By names and images, all powers are awakened and reawakened." A great example is thinking of love when you see a heart.

When you choose to charge your sigil, calm your mind while meditating and continue to look at your sigil while repeating your affirmation. Feel it's energy. Anchor that feeling and your affirmation to your sigil. Meditate on it. Meditate on your new reality and its' vibration.

If you choose to charge it through sexual energy, which is very powerful, look at it or think about it during an orgasm. Whichever way you decide to charge your sigil, you will not only attach this energy to this particular sigil, but you will also embed it and burn it into your subconscious mind.

Now that your sigil is ready, step number 4 is using it. The sky is the limit. Since it is very discreet and only you know the meaning, you can use it in so many ways! Unlike the written affirmation, which you might put away if a friend stops by because you would not necessarily want others to see something like "**I AM** enough", "**I AM** attracting my soulmate," or "**I AM** pregnant." Now go ahead and make it a screensaver on your phone, a background on your laptop, get a tattoo, get a keychain, engrave it on a pendant or bracelet, keep a picture of it in your wallet, or even draw it on your notebook cover. You will reawaken that energy every time you see, wear, and touch it.

The Law Of Assumption And The Use Of "I AM" Affirmations

The Law of Assumption is different from the Law of Attraction. The Law of Attraction says that like attracts like. It also states that you attract what you vibrate. So, you do not attract what you want; you attract what you are. In other words, you will not attract that new job or new house until you are worthy, specifically until you feel worthy. You will not manifest that car, that relationship until you are emitting the vibration of owning that car or being in that relationship. You will not be able to manifest that financial abundance before you start living that abundance in your mind first.

The Law of Assumption assumes that you already have what you desire. The Law of Assumption states that I will be so entirely certain that what I desire has already manifested that it will have no choice but to manifest into my reality. We all are born with desires, dreams, and goals. The Universe would not have given you desires if they were not possible to manifest. That dream, that vision, that desire was born in your heart for a reason. It has the potential to manifest in your life. The potential was born into you. All you have to do is choose to allow it to come from you. There are two mindsets to choose from. You can choose to have a positive attitude and think about numerous ways your dreams can come true, or you can choose a negative attitude and focus on the reasons and circumstances why this dream cannot manifest. You can always choose to either take an empowered and inspired action that will bring us one or many steps closer to your dreams or you can choose to sit back, do nothing, and complain.

Attitude has stopped way more dreams from manifesting than failure ever will. The Law of Assumption is an incredible mindset that can help you manifest all of your dreams and desires. Don't think of your goals; think from your goals and act "as if". When you live your life with certainty, intention, and clarity, you build that missing bridge between your dreams and reality. When you live with the conviction that your

Introduction

dreams have manifested, you summon the mighty creative forces of the Universe that take care of your manifestation.

Einstein said, "Reality is merely an illusion although it seems to be a very persistent one". You are the creator of your reality, and you decide how you want that reality to be. By focusing on different potentials, you create different realities. You live in this pulsating and vibrating Infinite Intelligence where everything is energy, and that energy emits different frequencies. Different levels of frequencies carry different levels of consciousness. Everything changes form, everything is one, and everything responds to your energy. What you desire already exists; it's already YOURS. It is happening somewhere on a different frequency than you are currently vibrating. Your task is to shift to a state where you believe nothing in this world can stop your manifestation from coming true.

Whenever you affirm something, you assume that you are already it. For example, you might say something like, "**I AM** my perfect weight," "**I AM** confident, well organized, and motivated," "**I AM** in a loving and committed relationship," "**I AM** healthy, fit, and have loads of energy," "My business is flourishing," "I live in the state of happiness, abundance and success." All the statements are in the present tense, as if they were already part of your reality. There is no "I wish…, I would love to…, maybe…, **I AM** going to…soon."

The affirmations are never used in the future tense. Future tense would say, "I will be in a happy and loving relationship," "I will buy my dream home," "I will manifest a perfect job opportunity." These all affirm your desires remain in the future. Future often implies uncertainty. There is always a possibility that things will either happen or not. Future affirmations create doubt and separation. According to the Law of Assumption, you cannot manifest something you are separate from or not sure about. The Law of Assumption removes all doubt of things not happening. It is CERTAIN that your desire is going to manifest.

You are convinced that your relationship HAS to get better than ever. You are convinced that you are going to be more successful than you have ever been. You are sure that the profit from sales this year will be the biggest it has ever been. You are confident that the house is going to sell. You are sure that you will be offered the position you applied for. You are absolutely sure that you will meet your monetary goals for this year.

All the affirmations you say also imply the end result and therefore are great tools to practice and implement the Law of Assumption. Law of Assumption affirmations assume the following, "I have already manifested," "I have already attracted," and "I have already created whatever I desire to attract." "Already" IS part of your life. It already HAS manifested on the different realms of consciousness, and now you are only creating a vibrational road for it to matriculate down to this physical reality.

The Law of Assumption states that whatever you desire to manifest - a s s u m e i t. For when you assume it, you become it. Imagination creates your reality. The secret to manifesting is to totally and completely assume that your desire is already yours. If you say, "I don't see my spouse/partner in my life," "I don't have the money," "I do not have the job," "**I AM** not healthy," "I don't have that car/house/apartment," that is because you are looking at it from a 3D perspective. Hence, you are not feeling your desire. Focusing on your 3D and outside circumstances will always make you feel the absence of manifestation. Concentrate on your dreams will help bring out the vibration of opportunity for manifestation. The Law of Assumption will help you to tune into the frequency where what you desire to manifest is already happening, where what you desire already exists.

Miracles

MIRACLES

Sometimes life becomes really difficult. Nothing seems to work for you. Everything seems to be falling apart, failure after failure after failure. Maybe you or your family member is dealing with cancer or another fatal disease. Maybe you are going through a breakup or divorce with your partner or spouse. Perhaps you have experienced the loss of your job, or your business has failed. You might be engulfed in debt. Perhaps you are going through depression. You might be in a toxic and abusive relationship. However, no matter your circumstances, it might be hard to see yourself getting into a better place mentally, physically, or financially. This is when you need a breakthrough, a magical turnaround; you need a MIRACLE.

These affirmations will help you focus on manifesting that miracle in your life. Use these affirmations in bed, just before falling asleep. Your subconscious mind will continue working on your intention and manifesting that miracle into your reality.

1. The Universe is full of magic and miracles, and I have the power to invoke them into my life.
2. I attract a smile; I attract an opportunity; I attract a miracle.
3. I love the energy of my miracle: I know how it feels; I know how it looks; I know how it smells; I tune into its frequency every day. My miracle feels amazing.
4. My miracle is easy for me, it is absolutely possible for me.
5. The happier **I AM**, the easier it becomes to manifest miracles. Happiness is magnetic, and it is a magnet to my miracles.
6. My miracle is manifesting. **I AM** ready for it. **I AM** patient, and I trust the divine timing.
7. Infinite Intelligence is my superpower; it has thousands of ways to manifest my miracle.
8. I believe in miracles; I create miracles.
9. Even if everybody around me says it is not possible, I choose and continue to believe in my miracle.
10. My heart and my soul feel that my miracle has manifested already.
11. **I AM** aligned with miracles. Miracles are part of my life now.
12. My desires become my miracles.

13. My body, mind, and soul are tuned into the vibration of miracles.
14. My heart is a magnet for miracles.
15. The Universe is a miracle. **I AM** the Universe. **I AM** a miracle.
16. Every night while I sleep, the Universe is working on my miracle.
17. I only focus on my miracle. I let go of everything that no longer serves me.
18. Every area of my life is filled with miracles. I allow them, and I accept them.
19. The Universe is blessing me with expected and unexpected miracles all the time.
20. I deserve the miracle that I desire.
21. Today and every day, I summon the mightiest energies of the Universe to create my miracle.
22. I believe that all the potentials exist already. My miracle has already manifested.
23. **I AM** patiently waiting for my miracle to unfold in physical reality.
24. My breakthrough is close, I can feel my miracle is about to manifest.
25. Miracles are flowing into my life.
26. Everything is possible for the Universe, and so is my miracle.
27. My belief is more than enough to manifest my miracle.
28. I see miracles and prosperity when I look in the mirror.

29. I see infinite positive possibilities in every area of my life.
30. **I AM** ready to receive my Miracle.
31. **I AM** ready to receive my blessings.
32. My energy travels through space and time bringing miracles into my life.
33. I attract miracles because I believe in Miracles.
34. I believe in the Universe and its infinite power.
35. **I AM** aligning with my miracle, so that it can manifest.
36. **I AM** one with my miracle. **I AM** my miracle.
37. I allow the magical power of the Universe to create miracles in my life.
38. The Universe is creating a miracle for me right now.
39. Miracles are ready to flow like a river into my life.
40. **I AM** expecting nothing less than a miracle. I CLAIM my miracle.
41. I have manifested so many beautiful miracles in my life; I CAN do it again!
42. **I AM** a miracle magnet.
43. I have the power to create a miracle in my life.
44. I ATTRACT miracles.
45. I CAN manifest anything; I CAN manifest MIRACLES.
46. My miracles are boundless.

47. Source Energy guides me toward my Miracle. I tune into my intuition, and I follow its guidance.
48. My attention is energy. I always CHOOSE to focus on my Miracles.
49. Miracles are part of my reality; I invite them to my life by believing in them.
50. **I AM** in the flow state. Miracles are flowing to me easily.
51. I welcome miracles with a grateful heart.
52. **I AM** worthy to witness miracles in my life; I can already feel their beautiful vibration.
53. **I AM** co-creating miracles with the Universe.
54. **I AM** creating the most amazing miracle in my life.
55. I summon the creative powers of the Universe. I CLAIM my miracle.
56. **I AM** sending out a magnetic intention, and the Universe grants me a miracle.
57. The Universe is creating miracles all the time.
58. **I AM** tuning into the vibration of miracles.
59. I align my heart with the frequency of Miracles.
60. **I AM** a living magnet, and I attract miracles into my life.
61. I believe with all my heart that the Universe is sending me a Miracle.
62. The Miracle **I AM** about to manifest will be far beyond what I expected.

63. **I AM** claiming my miracle; **I AM** invoking my miracle.
64. Miracles feel like joy, happiness, abundance, and freedom to do what I desire.
65. Miracles happen daily in my life.

Personal Empowerment

CONFIDENCE

Confidence and personal magnetism are the primary energies of the Law of Attraction. Your ability to manifest things into reality depends greatly on these two key factors. When you exude confidence and personal magnetism, you can easily attract people, things, and circumstances into your reality.

You become what you believe, and you believe what you affirm to yourself. A thought repeated over and over again becomes a belief. An affirmation repeated over and over again becomes a belief.

Your lack of confidence may also stem from your environment. Many of your limiting beliefs come from your childhood because your parents, caretakers, relatives, or teachers told you too often what you are not good at. They imposed their limitations, their fears, and their doubts on you. It is important, therefore, to go back and explore where your low self-esteem started and how these limiting beliefs were instilled in you. The next step is to challenge those beliefs, eliminate them and replace them with empowering beliefs and affirmations. For example, "I believe in myself," "I believe in my capabilities and skills," "I exude personal magnetism," "I feel incredible," "I feel wonderful," "I feel certain," "I feel confident," "I feel incredible," "I feel wonderful," "I feel certain," and "I feel confident."

If you start choosing confidence, practicing confidence, and aligning affirmations with your actions in everyday life, you will soon shift into a new reality.

It is also important to note that confidence is about fully accepting and embracing yourself just as you are. It's about breaking the vicious cycle of comparing yourself to others. You are unique, and there is no one like you. Every one of us has a unique blueprint and a life path. You are all simply incomparable, yet you always make comparisons. Comparing yourself to others slowly chips away at your confidence.

Below you will find many incredible affirmations for your self-confidence. Rehearse them while looking at yourself in the mirror. Smile! You can even put sticky notes on your mirror with your favorite affirmations. Keep reminding yourself of your greatness! Make "I've got this" your philosophy of life!

66. I breathe and inhale confidence and exhale timidity.
67. I enjoy being confident and meeting people.
68. **I AM** worthy of all the good things in my life.
69. **I AM** confident.
70. I confidently meet any challenge that **I AM** faced with.
71. **I AM** deserving of success and happiness.
72. **I AM** growing and changing to become the best version of myself.

73. I believe in myself.
74. I trust in my capabilities and skills.
75. **I AM** naturally confident.
76. I know my self-worth; my self-confidence is rising.
77. **I AM** strong and powerful.
78. **I AM** gaining confidence daily.
79. **I AM** magnetic and powerful.
80. **I AM** unbelievably confident and secure.
81. **I AM** attracting people to my magnetism and confidence.
82. I feel incredible, I feel wonderful, I feel certain, I feel confident.
83. **I AM** expanding my energy field in confidence and magnetism.
84. **I AM** unstoppable.
85. **I AM** filled with inner power.
86. **I AM** filled with unconditional love.
87. I believe entirely in myself, my skills, and my abilities.
88. I make wise decisions.
89. **I AM** full of incredible knowledge designed to ensure my success.
90. I feel complete within myself.
91. **I AM** a treasure.

Personal Empowerment

92. I aim to be my best version every single day.
93. **I AM** radiating positive vibrations from my energy field.
94. I think positive thoughts easily.
95. **I AM** master of my circumstances.
96. **I AM** always growing and evolving.
97. **I AM** grateful for each breath I take, for it is a gift for myself and others.
98. I trust my abilities completely.
99. I believe in my power totally.
100. **I AM** unique, and that is my strength.
101. **I AM** in demand.
102. **I AM** a magnet for personal power, harmony, and peace.
103. **I AM** always choosing to be confident.
104. **I AM** naturally confident.
105. **I AM** confident about what I say, how I, act and the way I show up every day. **I AM** doing my best.
106. **I AM** attracting many amazing things to my life with my magnetic confidence.
107. **I AM** always willing to try new things; I no longer shun challenges but welcome them. **I AM** confident that I can handle any situation.

108. I believe in myself and my future! I believe that great things are unfolding for me.
109. **I AM** enough in every way possible. **I AM** unique, talented, and **I AM** a gift to this world.
110. **I AM** my true authentic self. I stand tall in my personal power.
111. I honor myself; I embrace my flaws and rejoice about my strengths. **I AM** a great human being.
112. Everything is possible for me.
113. All I need is already within me; I tap into my inner source of confidence.
114. I always make the best out of any situation. **I AM** calm and confident.
115. I trust my intuition, and I trust my decisions.
116. My life matters. I make a difference in many people's lives.
117. I believe in myself and my power to create my best world.
118. **I AM** an unlimited spiritual being. Everything is possible for me.
119. I was sent to this Earth to accomplish great things. **I AM** confident about myself and my life.
120. I act with confidence even in challenging situations. I believe **I AM** capable of always finding the best solution.

121. I value myself. I respect myself. I love myself. I accept myself just the way **I AM**.

122. **I AM** growing, learning, and becoming a better version of myself every day.

123. **I AM** living with confidence and personal magnetism.

SELF-LOVE

Self-love is the start of Universal love. We know how to give love to others, but why do we struggle to open ourselves to receive it or give it to ourselves? Do loving and caring acts from others make you feel weird sometimes? Is it easier for you to love others and care for them than love yourself? It is because you are used to giving and giving and giving that you no longer know how to receive. You don't know how to receive it because you do not feel worthy of love even though you crave it more than anything.

I work with many people who confess they don't know how to love themselves. Few are ever taught this valuable skill. Most people have been taught to pour their love outward. You can be the most kind, loving, and caring person on Earth, but if you do not give some of that love to yourself, then that love is incomplete. You will not attract what you give but what you believe about yourself. Check that your beliefs about love will not attract unworthiness.

Self-love is many things. Empowering self-talk, setting boundaries, communicating your needs, saying "NO," taking time out when needed, smiling, doing things that make you happy, and educating yourself are all forms of self-love.

Personal Empowerment

I challenge you to start practicing self-love from this moment onward. Start with the affirmations. Get a lovely notebook, and every day religiously carve out some time to write the affirmations in your handwriting. Writing is very special and magical. It imprints your mind and body into the quantum field. Self-talk matters just as much. Say those incredible affirmations and fall in love with yourself!

124. I love myself unconditionally.
125. **I AM** enough. **I AM** more than enough.
126. **I AM** worthy of love.
127. **I AM** worthy of all the beautiful things life offers me.
128. I matter, and my presence matters.
129. **I AM** special, **I AM** unique, and I appreciate myself.
130. I accept myself just the way **I AM**.
131. **I AM** beautiful on both the inside and the outside.
132. **I AM** forgiving, kind, and compassionate with myself.
133. **I AM** patient and loving with myself.
134. **I AM** a gift to this world, and I make it a better place.
135. **I AM** understanding with myself; I forgive my mistakes. They allow me to grow.

136. I have my gifts and talents; I have my unique blueprint. **I AM** special, just like everybody else is.

137. I only compare myself with myself, and I always strive to be a better person than I was yesterday.

138. **I AM** at peace with my past decisions. I know I did the best I could at the time.

139. My heart is free, my mind is free, and my soul is free. I enjoy incredible freedom.

140. I take steps to empower myself and my life.

141. I enjoy treating myself in every way possible.

142. **I AM** opening my heart to welcome the incredible things I deserve.

143. I always encourage myself and cheer for myself when I need it.

144. I make unique decisions to gain wisdom.

145. **I AM** important, and I respect myself.

146. **I AM** happy with who **I AM**.

147. **I AM** always honest with myself.

148. I only make choices that work toward my highest self.

149. I choose my boundaries, and others always respect them.

150. I always set loving boundaries with others.

151. I mind my own interests just as much as I mind the interest of others.

152. **I AM** continually growing and evolving. My world is becoming more prosperous day by day.

153. I let go of my past, and **I AM** within the present moment embracing its beauty.

154. I came to this Earth to love, enjoy life, and accomplish great things. I enjoy and cherish every second of my journey.

155. **I AM** proud of my past self, and **I AM** proud of my future self that **I AM** becoming.

RAISING YOUR VIBRATION

Everything is energy; everything material and non-material is energy, and all energy vibrates at a particular frequency. We all vibrate at a higher or lower frequency, as does everything and everyone around us. I have a frequency, but so does the couch I sit on. Every frequency carries information.

Your power as a manifestor and as a co-creator depends on your vibration. It will determine what exactly you will be able to attract to your life. You will only attract your desire when you become a vibrational match to what you want to manifest. Everything manifests when you are aligned and tuned into the frequency of your desire.

This is why getting your vibration raised to the level of whatever you desire is CRUCIAL. This is the key to money, love, health, success, or anything else. The Law of Attraction is a sub-law of the Law of Vibration. Your beliefs, attitudes, perceptions, thoughts, feelings, and emotions determine your vibration. They can be conscious or subconscious.

The better you feel, the higher your vibration. So, you will attract (The Law of Attraction) what you vibrate (The Law of Vibration). The happier, more joyful, loving, and expansive you feel, the more wonderful things, people, and situations will vibrate into your life. On the other hand, the gloomier you are, the more 'in need' you are; the more negative people, things, and situations you will attract into your life.

You are the gatekeeper to your mind; therefore, always choose to entertain only empowering and resourceful thoughts. When you hold a thought, you emotionalize it; then, you start vibrating it. Use the affirmations below to raise your vibration and attract amazing things. Remember, you are ALWAYS attracting!

156. I always focus on what I desire. My attention is an invitation. I only invite things that I desire.
157. **I AM** filled with inner power.
158. I feel complete within myself.
159. **I AM** unique, and that is my strength.
160. I totally believe in myself, my skills, and my abilities.
161. **I AM** capable of creating incredible things.
162. No matter how challenging the situation is, **I AM** always able to handle it with grace and love.
163. I make wise decisions; **I AM** always intentional and compassionate.
164. I have the power to break my state and shift my vibration.

165. **I AM** the master of my thoughts; I consciously choose which thoughts I want to entertain.

166. Resourceful thinking manifests resourceful results.

167. **I AM** at peace with everything that happens around me.

168. **I AM** grateful for all the blessings in my life.

169. **I AM** choosing love, peace, and joy. **I AM** choosing to be unconditionally happy.

OVERCOMING BLOCKAGES

When manifesting, you can face different blockages, but the most prevalent ones are always in your mind. Your thoughts and your beliefs are the foundation of your manifestations. In order to overcome them or dissolve them, you have to work with your limiting beliefs to replace them with empowering beliefs. Your beliefs create your reality: Henry Ford said, "Whether you believe that you can or can't, you are right". Your beliefs will determine whether you will succeed or fail.

You will also have to look at your habits because they shape you more than you believe or realize. Procrastination, overthinking, negative thinking, being in your comfort zone, lack of discipline, impatience, and tendency to store physical and mental clutter are a few qualities that need examining.

At any moment, you can choose to let go of everything that no longer serves you. Your breakthrough is in your hands. Start practicing empowering beliefs and affirmations, then align them with empowering habits.

There is only one person that can change your life and manifest every goal and dream you hold in the silence of your heart. That person is YOU. So, choose to get out of your own way and own your power.

170. **I AM** choosing new positive habits.
171. **I AM** a product of new positive beliefs.
172. **I AM** patient, and I trust in God's plan.
173. **I AM** a master of my life plan.
174. **I AM** open to the spiritual lessons that **I AM** learning.
175. **I AM** in control of my emotions and feelings.
176. **I AM** dedicated to positive actions.
177. **I AM** devoted to positive beliefs.
178. **I AM** dedicated to releasing that which no longer serves me.
179. **I AM** welcoming opportunities for growth into my life and concurring all challenges.
180. **I AM** free now from old limiting beliefs. **I AM** open and ready to receive new blessings.
181. I no longer stand in my own way. **I AM** on a mission to empower myself.
182. I welcome change, I welcome new habits, I welcome new beliefs. They are all part of who **I AM** now.
183. **I AM** brave, wise, and confident enough to step out of my comfort zone.

SELF-EMPOWERMENT

Have you ever thought about what do the words self-esteem, self-respect, self-love, and self-empowerment have in common? The word "self." This seemingly short word makes a big statement that most seem to miss or get wrong. Humanity seems to struggle with everything that should normally come naturally from INSIDE.

However, it seems like unless validation, love, respect, and acknowledgment come from the outside; personal self-love, self-respect, and self-esteem cannot be felt on the inside. However, the word "self" is a beautiful indicator that all these great things are inside of us.

Remember, at the end of your journey, "self" is the only person you have to answer for. Everyone has an opinion about what is best for your life, but only you can experience the wonderful feeling of doing what makes you feel your best. It is time to set the bounders in your life to operate out of your self-identity before changing your life to fit their opinions.

When was the last time you told yourself, "**I AM** proud of you," "You did great," or "I know you did your best"? Stop waiting for encouragement from the outside, and be your own hero! Be your own light, be your own cheerleader, and be your own source of happiness. All you need to do is to focus on the positive attributes and qualities. When you focus on positive outcomes, you will find positive outcomes grow in your life. How about you start with "**I AM** unique, and **I AM** a gift to this world"?

184. **I AM** always learning and growing.
185. **I AM** living in a state of happiness, abundance, and success.
186. **I AM** deserving of a good life filled with abundance, love, and health.
187. I AM confident, smart, and intelligent.
188. **I AM** always growing and changing for the better.
189. **I AM** in love with the person **I AM** becoming.
190. **I AM** letting go of the negative feelings about myself.
191. **I AM** the goodness within myself.
192. **I AM** worthy of all the good things coming my way.
193. I acknowledge **I AM** a rising star.
194. **I AM** unique, and **I AM** a gift to this world.
195. **I AM** making people's lives better by contributing my unique power.
196. **I AM** a leader, and others are inspired by me.

LIFE PURPOSE

Let the Universe guide and connect you to your life purpose. Receive your soul's mission. Be curious, be proactive, and be ready to explore. Be prepared to listen to your intuition and not your EGO. Ask yourself, "What makes my heart sing?" Ask, "What are the things that **I AM** passionate about? What inspires me, and what ignites a fire in my eyes and heart?" Most importantly, ask, "When **I AM** gone, what legacy would I like to leave?"

What would you do if you knew you could not fail? Follow your heart; it knows the way; it will show you the way. There is a song in each of us that we need to sing. Create your soul's mission statement and practice together with these affirmations. Allow your life's path to unfold at its own pace gracefully. You can also write a letter to the Universe using affirmations that you will find in this book or create your own, to help you ascertain your life's purpose.

197. **I AM** a powerful force for truth, justice, and goodness in the world.
198. **I AM** on the perfect path for me and my desires.
199. **I AM** worthy of all things beautiful and wonderful.
200. **I AM** being guided by Source Energy to find my purpose.

201. **I AM** in accordance with my unique values and beliefs.
202. **I AM** a strong, persistent survivor.
203. **I AM** always focused on attracting a joy-filled life for myself and others.
204. **I AM** attracting incredible ideas through my creativity.
205. **I AM** in the right place and at the right time to live the life I desire.
206. I allow my life path to unfold at its own pace gracefully.
207. **I AM** overcoming every challenge in my life as it is a stepping stone to my bright and happy future.
208. **I AM** grateful for every situation that makes me grow and allows my soul to expand. Every step brings me closer back to my true self.
209. **I AM** here to serve others and to become the best and most empowered version of myself.
210. **I AM** here on this Earth to share the gifts God has generously given me.
211. **I AM** here to thrive; **I AM** here to love; **I AM** here to leave a beautiful legacy.
212. My life is amazing, and **I AM** grateful for it.

Love & Relationships

HEALING YOUR ROMANTIC RELATIONSHIP OR MARRIAGE

You can use the Law of Attraction to change the energy of your relationship. Affirmations are a great tool for changing the dynamics of your relationship. Affirmations will bring out and attract more of the energies currently missing in your relationship. When a breakup happens, the people in the relationship fall out of alignment with each other. At the beginning of your relationship, everything is in the flow because, naturally, you tend to show your best side and focus on the best qualities of your partner. Yet, as time passes, everyone tends to focus more and more on the things that do not work that irritate us. Guess what happens in this state; you attract more of it.

The secret is to place all of your attention and focus on the things that you desire. So, make a list of how you desire your relationship to be. Ask yourself, "What do I need to become to attract what I desire?" Consider thoughts like, "How do I become a container for what I desire?" or "What will I do differently this time?". Remember, the same behavior will give the same results. Are you at your full potential to develop and sustain a beautiful relationship? If the answer is "no", change your vibration. As you start making changes, you start vibrating at a different frequency. You will be vibrating in a new reality.

So, you will be doing the affirmations, and at the same time, you will be taking actions that support your relationship. You will create a new experience that will now change your mind and create new ways of being. When you believe something different, you attract something different.

What do you believe about your relationship? I have worked with many people who desired to rekindle their relationship. However, the majority had a hard time believing they could do so. You cannot attract something you do not believe.

On a subconscious level, you have to learn to vibrate that your ideal person is the person you are. Understand this person loves you. Believe you love this person, that you are meant to be together, that whatever happened, whatever drew you apart, a greater force, a greater power, a greater energy is now pulling you back together.

Affirmations allow you to direct your focus and your energy toward what you desire. Choose a set of powerful affirmations and set them as your "default mode." This will allow you to instantly recognize and cancel all the disempowering thoughts that will surely come to your mind when you feel low and missing your partner. Use these affirmations to reconnect with the energy of your future relationship that you are building with your vibration and the vibration that already exists in the infinite field of potential. Use these affirmations daily to help you "ignore" the 3D reality and summon the energies you need to build a new bridge between the two of you.

213. I believe that the Universe always has a way of bringing us back together.
214. My spouse/partner and I are falling deeper in love with each other.
215. I know my spouse/partner loves me, and we have a great marriage/relationship.
216. Every day, in every way, my relationship/marriage is improving and we are building the most incredible relationship.
217. I appreciate my spouse/partner, and my spouse/partner appreciates me.
218. Love, commitment, passion, care, and respect are all present in my relationship.
219. Every day through our loving energies, our relationship becomes more and more empowered.
220. **I AM** in a stable, honest, and loving marriage/relationship.
221. **I AM** worthy of an honest, loving, and devoted partner.
222. The one I love also loves me; the one I desire also desires me.
223. **I AM** enjoying an incredible marriage/relationship.

224. Every day **I AM** filled with appreciation for my spouse for all they do to enrich our marriage.

225. **I AM** vibrating a love frequency that causes my spouse to fall deeper and deeper in love with me.

226. **I AM** dedicated to making my relationship with my spouse stronger and stronger.

227. **I AM** responsive to listen to my spouse's needs and goals.

228. **I AM** loyal and devoted to my spouse.

229. **I AM** receptive to supporting my spouse in their decisions.

230. **I AM** certain that our marriage is growing stronger and stronger.

231. My spouse and I live a life filled with gratitude.

232. **I AM** grateful for my marriage/relationship.

233. **I AM** the biggest supporter of my spouse's talents and creativity.

234. **I AM** in love with my spouse unconditionally.

235. Our marriage is growing stronger and more passionate as each day passes.

236. **I AM** irresistible to my spouse.

237. **I AM** building a magical empire with my spouse.

238. I believe completely and totally in my marriage.

239. **I AM** a magnet for love, passion, and romance; **I AM** on the mind of the one I desire.
240. I know I have the ability to attract anyone that I desire.
241. The person I love sees me as a source of joy, happiness, love, and romance.
242. Every part of my mind, and soul is melding together with the one I love and adore.
243. I have deep telepathic communication with the one that I love.
244. Any past resistance to our loving union is fading away; nothing stands in the way of our relationship.
245. We are falling deeper in love with each other day by day.
246. I have the power to attract a specific person.
247. **I AM** love, and **I AM** in love.
248. No matter what has happened in the past, we are now sharing a really strong, loving, committed relationship.
249. I accept that **I AM** completely loved and adored by the one I love.
250. Whatever tears I may have shed in the past, **I AM** filled with love, bliss, and happiness now because **I AM** with the one I love.
251. **I AM** telepathically connected to the one I desire. The one I desire is telepathically connected to me.

Love & Relationships

252. **I AM** on my lover's mind. **I AM** always on my lover's mind.
253. I love that my relationship is growing day by day. We are falling deeper and deeper in love. I feel good being with the one that I love.
254. I draw my lover to me like a bee is drawn to honey.
255. I love my partner, and my partner loves me.
256. The one I love is drawn to me magnetically.
257. I happily give and receive love each day.
258. I only attract a healthy, loving relationship.
259. **I AM** like a magnet for the person that I desire.
260. Our relationship grows and expands day by day.
261. **I AM** easily attracting my lover into my life.
262. **I AM** attracting my dream future and my dream relationship.
263. **I AM** confident the one I desire is falling in love with me more and more.
264. Our love is growing so strong.
265. **I AM** loved.
266. I love the fact that my lover is always thinking about me and texting me.
267. Our desires grow stronger and stronger each and every day.
268. **I AM** attracting a specific person to my life for a life of incredible love.
269. I have attracted the lover of my dreams.

270. My partner sends me loving messages all day long.
271. **I AM** falling deeper in love with my lover, and my lover is falling deeper in love with me.
272. **I AM** always on the mind and in the heart of my lover.
273. **I AM** irresistible to my partner; my partner only wants to be with me.
274. We are building a new bridge between us. It leads us to a loving, passionate, and fulfilled relationship.
275. **I AM** the perfect partner for my lover/spouse.
276. My spouse and I are committed to building together the most amazing relationship.

ATTRACTING YOUR SOULMATE

These powerful affirmations will help you to become magnetic to your soulmate and attract them into your life. When working on a relationship, whether you are looking to rebuild a relationship, improve your current relationship, or meet your soulmate, it is important to increase your vibration of love. Unconditional love is the purest and highest frequency that you can attain as a human being. If you want to attract love, you must become love. When you are at the frequency of love, your mantra becomes "**I AM** lovable," "**I AM** loved," and "**I AM** grateful for all the love that I have in my life."

Please bear in mind that your soulmate is out there manifesting you as well. He/she is looking to find you and meet you, just as much as you desire to meet her/him. As you align with your heart's desire and the vibration of love, the Universe will create the opportunity for the two of you to meet.

These affirmations bring your heart to a new place of love, openness, and passion. They will raise your vibration to a higher consciousness in the frequency of love. Do these affirmations for 28 days, a complete lunar cycle, to completely transform your energy field. You will be a magnet for love, passion, and the best relationship you could ever imagine with your soulmate.

277. **I AM** always attracting the love of my life.
278. **I AM** attracting my soulmate.
279. **I AM** magnetic; therefore my soulmate is deeply attracted to me.
280. My heart is open to happiness, joy, and love.
281. **I AM** attracting the love of my life always, in every way.
282. With each breath I take, the one I love and I are coming closer together.
283. I trust in the Universe and in my vibration to attract my soulmate.
284. I truly believe the Universe has my back and that my relationship is melding together closer and closer.
285. **I AM** worthy; **I AM** enough for the one I love.
286. I love my soulmate.
287. There is only flow, a wonderful flow of loving energy between my soulmate and me.
288. My heart is open to possibilities of all kinds.
289. **I AM** attracting the love of my life deeper into my life.
290. **I AM** attracting my twin flame into my life for love, joy, happiness, bliss, romance, and passion.

291. My soulmate and I are melding closer and closer together: our hearts, our minds, our bodies, our souls.

292. I trust in my vibration to attract the one I love.

293. **I AM** fearless. **I AM** calm and relaxed. **I AM** safe and secure. **I AM** blessed with unconditional love.

294. **I AM** destined to be with my soulmate.

295. **I AM** attracting the love of my life always in every way.

296. **I AM** worthy of incredible love.

297. I know that my soulmate is out there manifesting me.

298. **I AM** sharing an incredible heart-to-heart, soul-to-soul connection with my soulmate.

299. **I AM** irresistibly magnetic to my soulmate. I draw my soulmate to me.

300. I open my heart to love, passion, and happiness. **I AM** worthy of living the most beautiful and fulfilling love.

301. I vibrate unconditional love, and I attract unconditional love. **I AM** attracting my soulmate.

302. Every day the attraction between my soulmate and I grows stronger.

303. My soulmate and I share an incredible bond; time and distance are immaterial.

304. **I AM** closer to my soulmate every day.
305. I follow the guidance of my higher self because it knows the way to my soulmate.
306. My soulmate is the answer to my unspoken prayers.
307. My soulmate is the answer to the calling of my soul.
308. I allow love to flow to me and through me. **I AM** love. **I AM** loved.
309. My soulmate and I share the deepest connection. Love is our language.
310. My soulmate is my friend. My soulmate is my lover. My soulmate is my source of unconditional love.
311. **I AM** creating space for my soulmate in my heart and my life. **I AM** ready to experience the most incredible love.
312. **I AM** creating an abundance of love in my life.
313. Love is present in every area of my life. Love is present in my body, mind, soul, and spirit.

ATTRACTING YOUR PERFECT RELATIONSHIP OR MARRIAGE

Get clear and specific on what you desire to manifest. Is it a relationship, or do you want to attract marriage? If your heart desires to get married, then focus on marriage, not just a relationship. A relationship is a step toward committed marriage. If marriage isn't what you want, if you just want a relationship then focus on that. Focus on what it feels like; living together, loving together, and growing together. If marriage is what you desire, stop trying to simply attract a relationship and then see if you can "upgrade it into a marriage". Be intentional about your ultimate manifestation goal.

It is also important to have a clear vision of what you desire out of your marriage or your relationship. What is it that you deeply desire to receive on a daily basis in your marriage or relationship? More importantly, what do you deeply desire to give to another person for the rest of your life? Get specific. Start with what you wish to give first because it will shift you to a higher level of consciousness. If you are grieving, now you will be thinking in terms of unconditional love. Complete the energy by next thinking about receiving. All healthy relationships have a cycle of giving and receiving.

Get CRYSTAL CLEAR on what you desire. You have the right to desire whatever speaks to you, a marriage or a relationship. Your relationship is not a community project with your family and friend. Your relationship or marriage has to make sense to you and only you. Different marriages look for different things; different relationships look for different things. Don't try to adopt somebody else's vision or fit their relationship framework. What rocks your boat? What feels good to you on your journey?

Your clear intention is like a lighthouse in the dark that shows the way to your soulmate, partner, or future spouse. Many people want to attract their soulmate and be in a loving relationship, but they are unable to describe what looks like, what it feels like, and what is important to them in their perfect relationship. Clarity creates certainty. It also creates magnetism for your specific person. Think of clarity as a laser beam. It's sharp and focused. Without clarity, you are attracting everything and everybody into your life because you want to attract a "relationship" or a "soulmate". Now with clarity, you have made space for a very specific kind of relationship and a certain type of person. Now you will be broadcasting the vibration of the relationship or marriage you desire with a very specific energy. This energy will have the Universe bringing you exactly what you asked for.

Start practicing these affirmations for the marriage you desire. Do it consistently on a daily basis until you meet your perfect partner. Use this section hand-in-hand with the affirmations on attracting your soulmate. Also, use the advice provided there.

Love & Relationships

314. **I AM** happy in my relationship.
315. **I AM** always ready to be loved.
316. **I AM** thankful to have found someone special.
317. **I AM** attracting love and commitment.
318. My soul is always open to love and happiness.
319. **I AM** followed by love on my life journey.
320. **I AM** experiencing love everywhere I go.
321. **I AM** magnetic and irresistible to the one I love.
322. My relationship is growing in every possible way, and it is fulfilling for both of us.
323. **I AM** experiencing love in my life with ease.
324. **I AM** thankful to God for all the love in my life.
325. **I AM** in a perfect relationship for me.
326. Love flows with ease into my life.
327. **I AM** so thankful that now **I AM** with the one I love.
328. **I AM** surrounded by love and happiness.
329. **I AM** filled with love.
330. The more I love myself, the more others love me in return.
331. **I AM** attracting perfect love.

332. **I AM** a magnet for love.
333. **I AM** very grateful for all the love in my life.
334. **I AM** always attractive to my lover.
335. **I AM** joyful when **I AM** with my partner.
336. **I AM** aware I have more love than possible.
337. **I AM** lovable and worthy of love.
338. My heart, soul, and thoughts are always open to love.
339. **I AM** always attracting love.
340. **I AM** a radiator of love.
341. I always attract a perfect relationship.
342. I welcome love into my life.
343. Love is attracted to who **I AM**.
344. I attract love easily everywhere I go.
345. I radiate unconditional love.
346. **I AM** living in the soul of love.
347. **I AM** happy and in love.
348. **I AM** worthy of love.
349. I enjoy a healthy relationship of love with myself.
350. Love surrounds me everywhere I go.

Love & Relationships

351. **I AM** unique. I love being myself.
352. I know the love of my life loves me.
353. **I AM** attracting the perfect lover for my life right now.
354. The one that I seek is seeking me.
355. **I AM** filled with gratitude for all the love in my life.
356. I spread love to all those I come in contact with.
357. My love is infinite.
358. I have discovered the love of my life.
359. **I AM** releasing everything standing in the way of love constantly.
360. Love is always flowing to me. Love is unlimited.
361. I love living a life of love.
362. I love my relationship.
363. I celebrate myself. **I AM** happy to love.
364. **I AM** forgiving to my partner.
365. I speak and love comes to me effortlessly.
366. As my desire grows for someone, they become more attracted to me.
367. Today and every day, I choose love. I choose passion. I choose joy.
368. **I AM** love. **I AM** loved. **I AM** in love.
369. My spouse and I love each other unconditionally.

370. Our relationship/marriage is filled with love, passion, commitment, respect, understanding, and adventures.

371. The more I open my heart to love, the more love is attracted to me.

372. **I AM** opening my heart to allow for more love to attract to me.

373. **I AM** loved, safe, and happy with my partner.

374. **I AM** in a loving, committed, exciting, and passionate union.

375. Every morning when I wake up, I give thanks for my amazing husband/wife.

376. My spouse brings so much love and joy to my life. **I AM** so grateful to have met him/her.

377. **I AM** happy, married, and **I AM** in love.

378. We always bring out the best in each other.

379. My husband/wife is a blessing. Our loving union is a blessing.

380. **I AM** attracting a committed relationship with my partner.

381. **I AM** happily married to my soulmate.

382. I love being married! I feel safe, secure, and loved.

383. My spouse inspires me to be a better person every day.

384. **I AM** with the most special, caring, loving, and devoted partner.

385. I adore my spouse/partner, and my spouse/partner adores me.

Love & Relationships

386. We always do our best for each other.
387. Our marriage is filled with unconditional love for each other.
388. Every day our relationship is growing stronger and stronger.
389. **I AM** magnetic to my partner.
390. My partner and I desire to spend the rest of our lives together.
391. My partner sees me as a source of love, support, inspiration, and passion.
392. **I AM** enjoying a healthy, loving, and stable relationship.
393. I feel special and appreciated in my relationship/marriage.
394. My partner is attentive, loving, and committed.
395. We are committed to our relationship/marriage.
396. Our marriage is a beautiful commitment to each other today and every day.
397. We both desire to be/live in a loving and committed marriage/relationship.
398. **I AM** the holder of the power to attract a specific person to my life.

MANIFESTING PREGNANCY

Use these incredible affirmations to open yourself to the potential of conceiving and letting go of resistance that most women encounter when they cannot conceive. In order to receive, you must tune into the vibration of receiving. Yet when you focus on a desire a lot, you tend to tune into masculine energy and hence the vibration of chasing. This creates a cycle of the more you resist, the more it persists.

Using these daily will allow you to take a step back, let go, and tune into the gentle feminine energy that exists within you. The feminine energy is the energy of nourishing and receiving. These will help put your body and mind at ease and connect with the frequency and the state of you carrying a new life in you. You can combine these pregnancy affirmations with appropriate healing affirmations to make them even more powerful.

399. **I AM** fertile and getting pregnant is easy for me.
400. My mind-body connection is strong. Whenever **I AM** ovulating, it is easy for my body to get pregnant.
401. **I AM** totally relaxed and free from worry because my reproductive system is strong and healthy.

Love & Relationships

402. **I AM** directing positive energy to my reproductive organs.
403. **I AM** creating life and ready to be pregnant.
404. **I AM** a strong, healthy, fertile woman.
405. **I AM** naturally fertile.
406. I can easily get pregnant.
407. Pregnancy is the most natural thing in the world, and I get pregnant easily.
408. I have a naturally strong reproductive system, so getting pregnant is easy for me.
409. My body is ready for pregnancy.
410. My body is ready to welcome the most precious gift of giving life.
411. I love being pregnant.
412. I love carrying a bundle of love and light in me.
413. I relax and let go of trying. I know that the Divine is about to bless me with a new life.
414. The Universe is expanding itself through my body and the life **I AM** bringing to earth.
415. I trust my body and its capacity to conceive.
416. I summon my creative energy to ignite this tiny spark of human life.

417. I AM patient, calm, and graceful as I conceive a baby. I trust the Divine timing.
418. I visualize myself surrounded by white healing light. It heals my body and prepares it to welcome my baby.
419. I lovingly release all my fears and doubts about my age and health. Pregnancy is easy for me.
420. **I AM** in sync with Universal timing. I allow it to choose the perfect time for me to conceive.
421. My body is amazing. My body is healthy. My body is capable of creating the miracle of life.
422. My fertility is increasing together with my intention to have a baby.
423. I have the power to control my fertility. I choose to conceive.
424. I feel the flow of Universal Life Force in me and I use this energy to manifest my pregnancy.
425. I take care of my body, mind, and soul. **I AM** in a perfect alignment for pregnancy.
426. My healthy new lifestyle enhances my ability to conceive, and my fertility is increasing daily.
427. **I AM** loved, and I feel safe to conceive.

428. I awaken the creative forces in me, and I conceive with ease.

429. My pregnancy is special and enjoyable.

430. **I AM** ready to deliver a healthy baby.

431. **I AM** healthy and strong, and so is my unborn baby.

432. **I AM** relaxed, calm, confident, and enjoying the experience of my pregnancy.

433. **I AM** completely dedicated to providing my baby with a happy home environment.

434. I love being pregnant.

435. **I AM** pregnant, and I feel beautiful.

436. **I AM** filled with abundance and pregnancy; they are one in the same.

437. I visualize myself enjoying an easy delivery.

438. I visualize myself at home, loving and playing with my beautiful baby.

439. **I AM** healthy, my baby is healthy, and my pregnancy is easy.

440. **I AM** becoming more attuned to the vibrations of my new baby, and my baby is becoming attuned to me.

441. **I AM** an amazing mother.

442. **I AM** ready to have a beautiful, healthy baby.

443. **I AM** so grateful that I have conceived a beautiful baby, and I appreciate the miracle of life.

444. **I AM** fertile, and getting pregnant is easy for me.

445. My mind-body connection is strong. Whenever, **I AM** ovulating it is easy for my body to get pregnant.

> Love & Relationships

GETTING OVER A BREAK-UP

These affirmations will promote your healing on all levels; physical, spiritual, and mental. As you use these affirmations, you will gradually let go of the past, focus on the present, and create an incredible future. Use these affirmations to help you to focus, appreciate what you already have, and stop mourning your past.

446. **I AM** healing. **I AM** feeling happier with every given second.
447. I trust the process of love and life.
448. I truly believe that the Universe has my back, and has the best in store for me no matter what.
449. **I AM** grateful for my relationship, and I have learned a lot making me ready for the right one.
450. **I AM** worthy, **I AM** enough, and **I AM** healing.
451. I love myself. I love my life. **I AM** grateful for all the experiences in my life.
452. Everything happens for a reason, and this heartbreak is only making me stronger.
453. **I AM** capable of feeling love again, **I AM** enough.

454. **I AM** comfortable being alone, but I will never be lonely as I always have my Divine spark.

455. **I AM** surrounded by love; everything is and will be okay.

456. I know this is just a part of my story, not my entire story.

457. **I AM** sure that everything is unfolding exactly the way it is meant to.

458. **I AM** opening my heart to all possibilities.

459. I gracefully let go of the pain. **I AM** making room for joy, peace, and wonderful new experiences.

460. **I AM** whole, **I AM** healed, **I AM** confident, and **I AM** open to all the amazing things that are lining up for me.

461. I look at my future full of amazing adventures, love, and magical moments. My future is bright.

462. I take the lessons and the wisdom that my relationship has taught me to manifest something amazing. **I AM** excited about my new journey.

463. I have wells of love, light and strength inside of me. I tap into my inner resources to heal and to rebuild myself.

464. **I AM** worthy of the best. **I AM** worthy of true unconditional love. **I AM** ready to welcome it to my life.

465. I love myself. I appreciate myself. I know, **I AM** doing the best I can today. Every day my heart heals a little bit more. **I AM** becoming my whole beautiful self.

HEALING YOUR RELATIONSHIP WITH A FAMILY MEMBER, FRIEND, OR COLLEAGUE

The vibration of these beautiful affirmations will help to build a new bridge between you and the person you fell out of alignment with. Compassion, forgiveness, and appreciation of what they did for you in the past will help you restore the natural flow of energies you shared before.

The ego can be bitter, but the spirit is naturally loving. Remember, you always decide which voice you choose to listen to. If you want to heal a relationship, any relationship, what you need to focus on is the good, loving, blessing that this person is.

Use these affirmations to put yourself in a higher vibrational state, to shift from being bitter about what happened, to rejoicing about reconciliation and being reunited. You can take a picture of that particular person or simply close your eyes and bring up his/her image and say the affirmations below. While you say the affirmations, send them love and gratitude.

466. **I AM** building a new and positive relationship with my specific person.
467. **I AM** grateful for all the fun we had and all the laughter we shared.
468. **I AM** grateful for everything that my specific person did for me.
469. **I AM** grateful to my specific person for all the times he/she was there for me.
470. I accept all people as they are without trying to change them. Instead, I tap into my inner source of compassion and unconditional love.
471. I always operate from a higher level of consciousness where lower vibrations like anger and jealousy are vanquished.
472. I always see other people through the eyes of compassion and unconditional love.
473. If I feel the need to change others, I know it is time to work on myself and fill my own cup with self-love.
474. **I AM** open to acceptance, understanding, and compassion.
475. I feel so much joy, happiness, and relief to have reconciled with (___). **I AM** grateful for our new relationship.

Love & Relationships

476. Unconditional love can heal everything and anything. I always choose love.

477. **I AM** forgiving. When I forgive, I make space for new energies and a completely new relationship.

478. Our relationship means a lot to me. I appreciate it, and I cherish it.

479. I exude love and peace, and I attract love and peace.

480. I always replace complaining with understanding, judgment with acceptance and compassion, egoism with selflessness, and hate or anger with love.

481. I have the power to create a compassionate and loving relationship with my specific person.

482. **I AM** the healer of my relationship through love and light.

483. I show my family and friends I love and care about them.

Money & Wealth

MANIFESTING MONEY

Money is energy and vibration. When you become the energy of money, you will find it easy to attract money into your life. You must start changing your frequency. In order to do that, you must change your programmed beliefs about money. If you change your beliefs, your thoughts will change. Changed thoughts will inspire you to take actions that are aligned with the vibration of abundance. Eventually, they will lead you to financial freedom.

Many people grew up believing that money is evil, money is scarce, money does not grow on trees, rich people are unkind, and money spoils people. You may have affirmations in your head like "You have to work hard to make your living," "You need to go to university to get a well-paid job," "The economy is bad," or "You need to come from a rich family or have connections to make it in this world."

The great majority of people do not have a healthy relationship with money. Therefore, at their core, they are not aligned with the vibration of abundance. When you think about money, do you feel bad, anxious and lower your vibrational or emotional state? What fears start to come up when you think about money? It is crucial, therefore, to rewrite your beliefs and programming to tune into the vibration of abundance. These money affirmations will help you on your journey. Start asserting the following statements: "**I AM** generously awarded for my work, skills, and knowledge," "Money flows into my life easily and without effort," "Money is easy to make," "I achieve my financial goals easily," "My financial abundance is growing every day," and "The Universe always provides for me."

Practice your money and wealth affirmations every day in every possible way. Every time you spend money, express your gratitude in a way like the following; "Thank you, every dollar I spend comes back to me multiplied." Every time you receive money, no matter how small the amount, express your gratitude. Say something like, "Thank you, I attract money from multiple sources," "I love manifesting money from expected and unexpected sources," or "Thank you, I love money, and money loves me." When shopping, even if you see an item you cannot afford right now, state in your mind "**I AM** grateful that I have more than enough money to buy everything that I desire." Do not tune into the vibration of poverty thinking; tune into the vibration of abundance thinking. When you see other people earning money, winning money, or receiving money, rejoice for them as if you were rejoicing for yourself. Soon you will say, "**I AM** always attracting the money and success that I desire."

484. **I AM** at an equal vibration with money.
485. I deserve wealth, abundance, prosperity, and money.

Money & Wealth

486. **I AM** worthy of all the abundance that I desire.
487. **I AM** manifesting money from an unexpected source.
488. **I AM** wealthy; **I AM** a money magnet.
489. Every dollar I spend comes back to me multiplied.
490. **I AM** abundant with money, assets, and wealth in all forms.
491. Every time I spend money, I bless it, and it finds its way back to me tenfold.
492. I love the creative power of money.
493. I have more than enough money. Money gives me freedom and allows me to live my life as I desire it.
494. Money is flowing like water into my life.
495. **I AM** always attracting the money and success I desire.
496. **I AM** surrounded by liquid assets.
497. I have multiple sources of income.
498. My ability to make large sums of money is constantly increasing.
499. I achieve all my financial goals easily.
500. **I AM** a money master.
501. Money is here to serve me. It is here to serve my dreams, my goals, and my desires.

502. I feel good having the money I desire.

503. **I AM** prosperous in all economic situations.

504. I choose to be wealthy.

505. **I AM** aware that money is too easy to make.

506. **I AM** rich, and I attract money.

507. Money flows easily into my life.

508. I love the vibration of money, and money loves my vibration.

509. **I AM** grateful for my increasing wealth.

510. **I AM** receiving money daily from a variety of sources.

511. **I AM** financially independent.

512. I love the vibration of money, because it responds to my desires.

513. **I AM** attracting unlimited amounts of money.

514. Money is good. I love the energy of money.

515. Every day, in various ways, money comes to me at the speed of thought.

516. Money is my servant. Money obeys my will.

517. Money is drawn to me like a powerful money magnet.

518. Money flows into my life easily and without effort.

519. I deserve wealth, abundance, prosperity, and money.

520. Money is easy to make. Money is easy to make. Money is too damn easy to make.

521. **I AM** worthy of prosperity, money, and financial abundance.

522. Money flows to me in miraculous ways.

523. I enjoy receiving money in many ways.

524. I love my positive, happy, and abundant life.

525. The happier I become, the more money I manifest.

526. The Universe has unlimited resources of money that I have access to.

527. Every day I get new inspiration on how to make more money.

528. I respect money and its energy.

529. I only speak positively about money and abundance.

530. The more money I spend, the more I receive back. The Universe rejoices in my abundance.

531. **I AM** open and ready to receive smaller and large amounts of money.

532. I invite money into my life by tuning into the vibration of abundance and wealth.

533. I always have different sources of money available to me. When one door closes, another one opens.

534. Every day, in every way, money is looking for ways to serve me.

535. Today and every day, I activate the vibration of wealth in me.
536. I love how money feels; I love how money sounds; I love how money smells.
537. Money is freedom, money is opportunities, money is joy; I welcome all that into my life.
538. I take action on amazing ideas that will help me to generate a lot of money.
539. I think, I feel and I act as if I already have all the things that I acquire with my new wealth.
540. **I AM** making money while I sleep. I love getting passive income.
541. **I AM** already abundant. I manifest, I attract, and I claim money!
542. My assets are growing and rapidly expanding. I flourish more and more.
543. I always make perfect investments. My gains are beyond my expectations.
544. Money is good. Money is a reflection of my positive vibes.
545. I always have more than enough money. I always feel abundant and grateful for the money I have.
546. **I AM** financially independent.

WINNING LOTTERY

Using these powerful affirmations, you can create opportunities for winning a lottery or any game of chance. Start using them at least 28 days before you expect any major win in your life. You will need to use them every night as you fall asleep. If you want to take your manifesting to the next level, do them every single day in the morning, throughout the day, and at night. When you become addicted to doing these affirmations, you change what your subconscious mind believes. When you change your beliefs, you change your thoughts; when you change your thoughts, you change your feelings and your outcome. The Universe gives you what you are, not what you want. Think of yourself as a prosperous and incredible being, and you absolutely will be one.

547. **I AM** so happy I won more money than I could ever spend.
548. I always knew that I was going to win the lottery!
549. Each day I attract more and more luck to my life.
550. **I AM** manifesting a steady stream of thousands and thousands of dollars.
551. Thank you, Universe, for blessing me with this huge amount of money. **I AM** grateful to have won all this money!

552. Choosing winning lottery numbers comes naturally to me.
553. I always win money. I appreciate the small wins and the big wins equally.
554. Money is attracted to me; money chooses me.
555. I love the happiness and freedom I feel every time I win money.
556. The Universe blesses me with large sums of unexpected money.
557. **I AM** a lottery winner. **I AM** a lottery winner. **I AM** A LOTTERY WINNER!
558. I love playing with the Universe: I love playing the lottery!
559. I attract large amounts of money into my life effortlessly and easily.
560. **I AM** magnetic to money. **I AM** magnetic to luck. **I AM** magnetic to the right circumstances.
561. **I AM** destined to win huge amounts of money.
562. **I AM** so happy to have won millions of dollars.
563. Winning money is easy and natural to me.
564. I love the feeling of security that money provides me. I no longer have to worry about my well-being.
565. My friends and family are beyond happy to see me win so much money.
566. I choose the winning numbers; winning the lottery is so much fun.

567. I love that the Universe blesses me with infinite amounts of unexpected money.

568. When I win, everybody wins - my family, friends, and people in need. I share my wealth because now I have more than enough money.

569. I cannot wait to experience all the adventures that the money I have won brings me.

570. **I AM** synchronized with Universal luck. **I AM** open and ready to receive my winnings.

571. **I AM** vibrating joy and excitement when I buy a lottery ticket because I know that **I AM** buying a winning ticket.

572. My amazing life is awaiting me with all the money I have just won!

573. **I AM** a magnet for prosperity and financial abundance.

574. I deserve to win the lottery. I believe **I AM** worthy to win the lottery. **I AM** open and ready to receive this unexpected blessing of huge amounts of money.

575. In my mind, I see heaps and heaps of hundred-dollar bills landing on my lap and in my account. **I AM** overwhelmed with joy and happiness to have won millions of dollars.

576. There is no limit to the amount of money I will win.

577.   **I AM** in alignment with the vibration of being a lottery winner. In my mind, **I AM** already living a financially abundant life.

Business & Career

HEALING YOUR BUSINESS

It's all about what you are telling yourself about what you are going through. You could be saying, "My business is failing," or, "**I AM** being presented with an opportunity to take my business to the next level." You can choose to focus on what is not working, or you can choose to focus on the opportunities you are being presented with. Look for ways to innovate, upgrade, and manifest new, inspiring ideas to help your business rise like that phoenix from the ashes with more power, energy, and potential than it ever had.

All business problems are created from a certain level of consciousness, and in order to solve, you have to rise to a higher level of consciousness. At a higher level of consciousness, you can see solutions, opportunities and create the pathway to take your business to the next level.

Once again, you must always focus on where you are going and where you want to be, what you truly desire and deserve. Always focus on the final destination, on your goals and dreams but not your current reality on your current situation. You should look at your circumstances but not give them more power and attention than they deserve. When you focus on your current reality, you only get more of the reality you are focusing on.

With the help of these affirmations, tune into the vibration of your business flourishing and being successful. See your business growing serve more and more people. Your business can only flourish with customers so why not to make it about them? Use affirmations that will help you to connect with the right customers. Send gratitude to your customers and watch your business grow.

578. **I AM** grateful for this opportunity to reinvent my business and take it to the next level.
579. **I AM** bringing new energies into my business.
580. I overcome all the challenges in my business and always come out stronger.
581. My business is strong and growing.
582. I transform challenges and obstacles into opportunities.
583. I used challenges as stepping stones to make my business even greater.
584. **I AM** transforming my business into something even greater.
585. Challenges of the past have given me valuable experiences; now I have the knowledge and experience to succeed.
586. My business is growing stronger and stronger day by day.
587. The effort and the energy I put in daily is paying off; my business is taking off again. Thank you, Universe.

588. Every challenge has a great solution. I tap into the potential of the solution to uplevel my business.

589. I love challenges, and I love the creativity that allows me to find out-of-the-box solutions.

590. My energy is the driving force of my business. I see my business flourish and serve many people.

591. Successful and supportive people are attracted to me and my business.

592. I always connect with the right people that add to making my business flourish.

593. I always attract the best customers.

594. My effort is always rewarded in the form of money and loyal clients.

Business & Career

MANIFESTING YOUR OWN BUSINESS

You are born with a lot of potential to create, advance, invent and surprise people. You have the potential to make not only your life, but other lives better too.

Every business has a calling. Whatever business you do, all the clients, all the people you will be working with, and all the people you will be interacting with will come to you for one special thing. Understanding that it will not be your product, services, or business offers; it will always be your ENERGY. There is something unique and special about each and every one of us. You might have the product customers seek, but they will return to interact with your energy.

You have to believe in what you are doing. You have to be passionate about what you wish to create. You have to be willing always to go that extra mile because that will always translate into the business.

You have remember, you will probably will never feel ready to embark on this journey. You will need to TRUST that everything works out in your best favor, and it will. All you have to do is keep tuning into the right potential. Practice these affirmations to open up to new business opportunities.

595. My business is flourishing.
596. **I AM** always creating and attracting excellent and profitable ideas.
597. The mission of my business is to serve people and to make their lives better.
598. I always meet the right people at the right time.
599. **I AM** always attracting new investors.
600. My business is constantly growing; my income is constantly increasing.
601. The Universe is protecting my business.
602. I always have enough liquid assets.
603. The number of clients is growing every day. The number of happy clients is exploding.
604. I easily attract my ideal clients. The right people always find me.
605. My business is beyond successful.
606. I skillfully use all the opportunities that come my way.
607. **I AM** blessed to be surrounded by honest business partners and generous clients.
608. I always have ideas on how to improve my business.
609. I love being independent and prosperous.

610. **I AM** filled with creativity, inspiration, and discipline. They allow me to create a great business concept.
611. **I AM** manifesting a great business idea. **I AM** manifesting business partners and resources needed to implement it.
612. I achieve all the goals I set for myself in business.
613. My profit is constantly increasing.
614. **I AM** aligned with my business, and **I AM** passionate about my product.
615. **I AM** growing together with my business.
616. **I AM** productive and successful in my business.
617. I love the energy of my business. It is a money magnet.
618. I love and enjoy the freedom that my business provides me.
619. **I AM** always respectful of others, and others are always respectful of my business.
620. My business has an excellent reputation.
621. My business is growing and developing very fast. **I AM** able to serve more and more people.
622. I have the best company in the world. My business gives me energy.
623. **I AM** always prepared for an opportunity.
624. The more money I invest into my business, the bigger return I get.

625. I turned my dreams into great ideas, and I turned my ideas into a business that is flourishing.

JOB/CAREER

Use these affirmations to strengthen your self-confidence, hone your skills, help you create, and attract that perfect job opportunity. Whether you are looking to change careers, find your first job, attract a new job, or simply to connect with your true potential, these affirmations will set you up for success in every possible way.

You can speak or write them at any time of the day. You can also use them just before sending your job application or doing an interview. Speak, write, and visualize your affirmations and watch your new career become your reality.

626. **I AM** manifesting my dream job. **I AM** so excited.
627. **I AM** always open to new opportunities to find my dream job.
628. **I AM** highly confident in myself and in my abilities to perform at my dream job.
629. **I AM** worthy of doing a job that I love.
630. It is easy for me to shine at my dream job interview.

| Business & Career |

631. Every career move that I make turns out to be a magical experience.

632. **I AM** a career magnet. **I AM** attracting excellent job prospects all the time.

633. **I AM** being paid very well to do an exciting and rewarding job.

634. **I AM** now attracting the perfect career for my talents.

635. **I AM** so happy and grateful for the new Dream Job that I have found.

636. The Universe is making all the perfect arrangements for my dream job.

637. The Universe is leading me to my dream job.

638. My career is soaring heights.

639. **I AM** highly valued, well thought of, and very skillful at what I do.

640. My job provides me with the opportunity to do what I love.

641. **I AM** helping other people, doing what I love.

642. My job is so much more than just something I enjoy; it is my soul's path. It's part of my mission on this Earth.

643. Every morning when I open my eyes, I thank the Universe for being able to do what I love.

644. **I AM** aligned with my perfect career.

645. I have the perfect career for me. I love what I do.

646. The happier **I AM**, the more I earn.

647. I have no limits to what I can achieve professionally.

648. My job gives me incredible opportunities to grow professionally.
649. I work in a positive environment. Every day **I AM** happy to give my best because I receive the best.
650. **I AM** a career magnet; I always attract excellent opportunities.
651. **I AM** aligned with the vibration of my perfect job. I welcome it into my life.
652. I deserve of the job I desire.
653. Job opportunities are flowing into my life. I select the best and most suitable job for me at this moment in time.
654. My job is a source of money, positive energy, professional and personal fulfillment.
655. I deserve to work at an amazing company with the best colleagues ever.
656. My skills are sought after. **I AM** highly valued in the job market.
657. I let go of my limiting beliefs over my career. I believe that I deserve the best.
658. A perfect job opportunity has been created for me. I welcome it.
659. I enjoy the hiring process. It is easy and fun.
660. My job interviews always go smoothly.
661. **I AM** confident that **I AM** the best candidate for my dream job.

Business & Career

662. **I AM** creating a perfect job opportunity for me.

663. I have found a lucrative activity that is a perfect match for my talents.

664. My new job is everything I have ever dreamed of; high salary, amazing team, and opportunity to grow.

665. My skills and efforts are always generously rewarded.

666. I love waking up in the morning because I love what I do.

667. Through my career, I share my gifts with the world.

668. I LOVE my job. I love what **I AM** doing.

669. **I AM** always open to new opportunities to find my dream job.

670. Interviewing is easy because I know **I AM** just meeting my new co-workers.

Success & Abundance

ATTRACTING SUCCESS

Don't focus on the obstacles; focus on opportunities. Every challenge you face is an opportunity to grow, expand, and improve. Always focus on the potential. Focus on the most empowered, fulfilled, and successful version of YOU that you can possibly imagine. Create a vision of the future. Start focusing on the qualities you would like to bring out in yourself. Affirm and speak them into existence.

671. **I AM** motivated to succeed.

672. **I AM** an achiever.

673. I deserve all the success flowing into my life.

674. I was born successful; it is who **I AM**.

675. **I AM** becoming more successful every day.

676. **I AM** a powerful magnet for success in everything I do.

677. **I AM** worthy and deserving of success in every area of my life.

678. I trust in my unlimited potential for greatness. I know **I AM** worthy of unbelievable success.

679. **I AM** feeling abundant success.

680. I celebrate my personal success each and every day.

681. Success is easy for me because **I AM** successful.
682. **I AM** successful. My incredible fortune is the result of my clear vision and creativity.
683. **I AM** the master of my life. I always take the success path that leads to the highest version of me.
684. I bust through old limiting beliefs and attract greater amounts of success daily.
685. I love how whatever I touch becomes successful.
686. I choose to think from my goals and choose my absolute best.
687. **I AM** fearless and successful.
688. **I AM** a successful person who knows what I desire and always keep sight of that vision.
689. **I AM** patient to wait for my success and **I AM** disciplined to work for my success.
690. **I AM** entering nothing but success.
691. Success is the only outcome I entertain in my mind and my heart.
692. Each day my intuition guides me toward success.
693. My decisions and my actions are always successful.
694. **I AM** successful in all areas of my life.

695. **I AM** in a natural state of success always.

696. **I AM** the creator of my own success.

697. **I AM** able to accomplish amazing things.

698. I use my gifts and talents to create my success.

699. **I AM** passionate about what I do.

TO STOP PROCRASTINATING

Procrastination has destroyed many dreams, opportunities, and potentials. As a manifestor, you must be open to taking inspired action and being proactive. You want to take advantage of the window of opportunity created for you by the Universe.

Awareness is the first step to change. The second step is working on your mindset and building your mental resilience. Procrastination often involves doing something difficult, uncomfortable, or scary. Procrastinating on needed tasks is easiest when you do not feel ready for it. Fear of rejection or striving for perfection is frequently what makes it seem safer to procrastinate. Procrastination is a way to avoid the stress you feel about an upcoming task, a project, or a life event. It is a way to stay in your comfort zone.

Comfort zones are zone where a lot of dreams die. Action is the bridge between you and your dreams. Every action that you take, or don't will shape your destiny. At the end of the day, you want to be proud of yourself and know that you showed up and never gave up.

Life is happening for you, not to you. No matter how small, every action you take contributes to actively shaping your life.

Be dedicated to your dreams and goals, be dedicated to your health, your fitness, your relationship, your job, your business, and most importantly, yourself.

Practice the affirmations given below daily. Use them as often as you need to until you have a breakthrough. Use them until you switch from a procrastinator to a go-getter!

700. **I AM** a doer, and I love getting things accomplished.
701. I can focus and concentrate at will.
702. All the resistance to achieving my goals has vanished.
703. **I AM** ready to face any fears I have and achieve my goals.
704. **I AM** willing to explore uncharted territories.
705. I take charge and get things done.
706. **I AM** always moving forward and working on my goals.
707. Being proactive comes to me naturally.
708. Making things happen is just what I do.
709. **I AM** dedicated to my goals.
710. I let go of everything that no longer serves me.
711. Action is the only way to achieve my goals and implement change. I always choose action.

712. I have enough confidence and determination to do things now.

713. I have strong self-discipline, which helps me to accomplish things on time.

714. Every action I take, every task I accomplish brings me closer to my goals. I love implementing my goals.

715. **I AM** a successful person, and successful people accomplish tasks quickly.

716. I choose to always accomplish things on time.

717. I love being in charge; **I AM** willing to take action.

718. Money loves speed; success loves speed, and I LOVE speed!

719. Time is money, and I use my resources wisely.

720. **I AM** committed to accomplishing all the tasks on time.

721. I respect my time, and I respect other people's time.

722. **I AM** proud of myself that I always accomplish things well before they are due.

ABUNDANCE AND PROSPERITY

Abundance and prosperity always start in your mind. The Universe is abundant, and so are you. The problem is that you may not feel or do not believe that you are worthy of abundance. You may not even believe that you can manifest it.

These affirmations will help you tune into the frequency of being, doing and having anything and everything you desire. Infuse every affirmation you say with a strong feeling. Believe that abundance is your birthright. Believe that you are a mighty manifestor. Notice how your vibration gets higher, and your mind opens up to the idea that you deserve more. You believe you deserve to be abundant.

723. **I AM** filled with infinite possibilities.
724. **I AM** growing beyond my wildest dreams.
725. **I AM** uncovering hidden gems within my life each and every day.
726. **I AM** satisfied with who **I AM** becoming.
727. **I AM** the holder of all I need to manifest the abundance I desire.
728. **I AM** a magnet for the money I desire.
729. **I AM** grateful for all the good things that have happened in my life and are yet to come.

730. **I AM** worthy of money, abundance, and wealth.
731. **I AM** abundant in all areas of my life.
732. **I AM** transforming into a wealth magnet.
733. Every day **I AM** manifesting more and more amazing things.
734. I vibrate prosperity, and the Universe blesses me with considerable amounts of money.
735. I see miracles and prosperity when I look in the mirror.
736. I have the potential to manifest the most incredible life that I desire.
737. What I seek is seeking me; what I desire desires me.
738. **I AM** in alignment with my abundant goals and dreams.
739. I have the power to create the abundance and prosperity I desire.
740. **I AM** worthy of everything this life has to offer me.
741. **I AM** guided by a higher intelligence that protects me.
742. Every day **I AM** creating and attracting amazing opportunities.
743. **I AM** enjoying a life filled with abundance and prosperity.
744. **I AM** a magnet for abundance.
745. My beliefs, thoughts, and feelings create incredible prosperity.
746. **I AM** a quantum magnet for abundance and prosperity.
747. **I AM** attracting resourceful and abundant people into my life.

748. I open my heart and wallet to wealth & prosperity.

749. My net worth grows as my self-worth continues to grow.

750. I open myself up to prosperity, and I allow it to flow to me and through me.

751. **I AM** uncovering hidden gems within my life each and every day.

752. I have everything I need to manifest the abundance I desire.

753. **I AM** filled with unlimited abundance.

754. Prosperity flows into my life like a river of gold.

Health & Wellbeing

MANIFESTING PERFECT HEALTH

Dis-ease means that your body and mind are not at ease. Continuous stress, anxiety, anger, guilt, negative thoughts, shame, lower vibrational energies, emotions you did not process, painful experiences you brushed off, toxicity that affected you, suffering you experience, and all-around negativity will give disease a place to root. Holding on to all this dark energy can make you physically sick. Pain and illness are your body's way of communicating with you. It tries to draw your attention to something that needs to be released.

In the same way, your thoughts and emotions can make you sick, they can also heal you. I'm absolutely sure that you have already heard about the Placebo effect. Your thoughts have immense power. Disease exists on a certain vibrational level and at a certain level of consciousness. Disease can no longer exist, if you raise your vibration and stay in that vibrational state. Your body and your cells have the ability to self-heal and regenerate.

Help your body to heal by vibrating higher. Choose to think only empowering thoughts, entertain only best-case scenarios, and tap into the potential of you being healthy and radiant. Start every day by talking to your body and thanking it for the amazing job it does and for the healing process. Thank every cell of your body, and send love to your body. Appreciate and acknowledge its power to heal. Then top it up with affirmations such as, "I believe **I AM** already healed," "**I AM** so grateful for my healing," and "Every day my body is growing stronger." You can combine it with gratitude affirmations expressing gratitude for your life, the Universe, and abundance.

755. **I AM** healthy, full of energy and vitality.
756. Every cell of my body vibrates health.
757. My body is healing, my body is regenerating, and my body is creating perfect health.
758. **I AM** aligned with perfect health.
759. **I AM** enhancing my perfect health with my daily habits.
760. I fill my body with a glowing white light that heals and protects it.
761. I choose health today and every day.
762. I let go of everything that is in the way of my perfect health and my perfect alignment.
763. My body has the power to heal itself.
764. The illness only exists in the old consciousness. **I AM** shifting to a new state of being. **I AM** healthy.
765. I only think empowering thoughts. I raise in vibration, and I heal my body.

Health & Wellbeing

766. I vibrate health, and the Universe sends me healing.

767. My health is blossoming, and I have loads of energy.

768. My infinite intelligence is capable of infinite healing.

769. **I AM** stepping into higher vibrational energy, and my body is healing.

770. My higher self has the potential to cure any dis-ease in my body.

771. I inhale love; I breathe out illness.

772. Every day **I AM** sending love and light to the body parts that need healing.

773. **I AM** healing my body.

774. **I AM** bringing new life to my heart, lungs, and legs.

775. I believe **I AM** already healed.

776. My mind and my thoughts have the power to heal my body.

777. I visualize my body in perfect health, harmony, and alignment.

778. Every day in every way, **I AM** healing.

779. My body is growing stronger; my immune system is becoming stronger and stronger.

780. **I AM** healthy, happy, whole, and love it.

781. I love, and I respect my body.

PERFECT BODY WEIGHT

Your body is a physical manifestation of the kind of exercise you do, the foods you eat, and the thoughts you think daily. All these things combined create your body. Remember, your genetics do not limit you; you are only limited by the power of your mind. When you shift your dominant thoughts and those thoughts matriculate into your subconscious mind, you shift your alignment with the Universe, and you can create something NEW.

Every time you eat, whether you are looking to lose or gain weight or improve your health condition, bless your food and believe it is replenishing and nourishing your body. Your body is intelligent and is working in alignment with the affirmations that you are saying. Every time you work out or are being physically active, say your affirmations to reinforce the positive body image. Every time you see yourself in the mirror or become body or weight conscious, repeat those positive affirmations again. These affirmations will help you to reprogram your limiting beliefs and create the body you desire.

782. **I AM** letting go of all the extra emotional weight on my body.
783. I believe in my ability to become the best physical version of myself.

784. **I AM** choosing to put in the energy to manifest my best body shape.
785. **I AM** my ideal weight because I nourish myself properly.
786. Every day in every way, I shed all my extra weight and live in my best body.
787. I choose healthy options that are right for my body and soul.
788. **I AM** aware that my metabolism is getting faster every single day.
789. I attain and maintain my ideal body weight.
790. I always chew my food properly so that my body can digest it and take out the nutrients I need to lose weight.
791. My metabolism rate is at its optimum level, and this maintains my ideal body weight.
792. I have the power and confidence to achieve a healthy weight and shape.
793. My body becomes more and more attractive every single day.
794. I love my body therefore, I only put clean food into it.
795. **I AM** grateful for my body therefore, I take care of it.
796. **I AM** dedicated to making nutrition and healthy eating choices.
797. **I AM** losing all my extra body weight effortlessly.
798. My body is powerful, healthy, and full of vitality.
799. With every inhalation of breath I take, **I AM** filling my body with healthy weight energy.

800. My body craves delicious healthy foods.

801. I love the taste of fresh vegetables.

802. I radiate health and confidence.

803. I lose weight quickly and easily.

804. My body is filled with vitality, health, and confidence.

805. **I AM** nourishing the life force that flows through my body.

806. Every time I eat healthy foods, my confidence increases.

807. I love exercising my body.

808. Weight loss for me is easy.

809. I crave new and healthy foods.

810. Everything I do is healthy and positive.

811. My body is filled with vitality and love.

812. I easily accomplish all of my weight loss goals.

813. I love looking in the mirror because I love seeing how my body changes.

814. My soul is lighter, and my body is lighter. I no longer eat to numb my emotional pain. I eat to nourish and thrive.

815. I choose to eat highly vibrational foods.

816. **I AM** attracted to healthy food; I find it easy to make healthy food choices.

817. The more I advance in my journey, the easier it becomes for me to lose weight.
818. **I AM** my perfect weight now.
819. **I AM** losing weight naturally and effortlessly.
820. **I AM** inspired to eat well and to choose food that will help me to lose weight.
821. I bless my food every time I eat. **I AM** grateful for it.
822. **I AM** fit and strong; **I AM** beautiful in my own way.
823. **I AM** healthy and lean. I love how my new body feels.
824. I enjoy healthy food that raises my vibration, and makes me feel amazing about myself.
825. My body is happy to let go of the excess weight.
826. I create healthy behavior patterns around food.
827. Healthy food is my friend: it nourishes my body and gives it energy.
828. It is easy to make healthy food choices.
829. **I AM** healthy, glowing, and **I AM** my ideal weight.
830. I deserve to be the best and most beautiful version of myself.
831. **I AM** proud to be consistent in my weight lose journey.

832. I enjoy exercising because **I AM** aware of its wonderful benefits to my body.

833. **I AM** grateful to my body for its amazing transformation.

834. **I AM** letting go of all the extra emotional weight on my body.

835. I believe in my ability to become the best version of myself.

836. **I AM** choosing to be active in manifesting my best body shape.

837. **I AM** my ideal weight every single day.

838. Every day and in every way, I shed all my extra weight and become my best version.

Health & Wellbeing

REVERSING AGING

It is possible to reverse aging using the power of the Law of Attraction by using affirmations. The key is combining consistency and patience with high vibrational nutrition and exercise.

With the human body, it's about alchemy and transformation. You are a vibratory energy being. You are always changing and transforming. The study of epigenetics has proved that you can turn specific genes on and off by thought alone. What you say to yourself and about yourself has a huge impact on how you look, and it has an impact on your energy field. About 95% of your manifesting power comes from your subconscious, so start affirming and believing that you exude vitality. Believe that your cells have the power to regenerate, that you are reversing or at least slowing down greatly the aging processes in your body.

839. My body, mind, and soul are radiating health and longevity.
840. I emanate energy and vitality. I emanate life.
841. My soul has no age, and my body follows it.
842. The cells of my body are constantly regenerating.
843. **I AM** feeling amazing, and I look amazing; my age is just a number.

844. My skin is firm, my joints are flexible, my muscles are strong, my mind is sharp, and my memory is amazing.
845. **I AM** capable of reversing my aging and increasing my vitality every single day.
846. Every night, during my sleep, I restore my youth; I de-age and regenerate.
847. I activate my body's potential to rejuvenate itself.
848. Every single cell in my body is programmed to regenerate. **I AM** activating my superpower to stay forever youthful.
849. Together with the Universe, I co-create health, vitality, and an amazing appearance.
850. **I AM** young, **I AM** strong, **I AM** vibrant, and **I AM** an eternal human being.
851. Every cell in my body vibrates youth and vitality.
852. I have reversed the aging process; my body is rejuvenating every moment.
853. Nobody believes my biological age; I look and feel amazing.
854. My intention is always to feel and look younger than **I AM**.
855. I love the happy, youthful, and glowing person I see in the mirror every day.
856. The Divine part in me reverses my aging effortlessly. My cells have an innate ability to regenerate.

857. **I AM** forever young, energetic, beautiful and I radiate life.

858. **I AM** complimented all the time on how amazing and young I look for my age.

859. My body is young, my mind is young, and my spirit is eternally young.

Healing & Clearing

HEALING BETRAYAL

Be compassionate and patient with yourself. Healing involves grieving. A grieving period is always expected when you lose a person, a relationship, a trust, or a bond. Allow yourself to feel all the emotions, but stop idealizing the relationship that you had. There is a gap between who you think they are and who they truly are. Let go of the stories that are playing in your head. Hurting people tend to hurt others with betrayal. Give yourself a time limit of 20 minutes a day to feel the grief and then move on with loving yourself.

Check-in with your self-esteem and self-respect. Betrayal can make you think it has to do with you, but it only has to do with the other person. You will never be enough for the wrong person. Take time to practice self-love and self-empowerment. Spend a lot of time with people that you trust. Be sure they love you, and you love them. People that uplift you and inspire you will help you heal. Believe that what's coming is better than what's gone because it is.

I suggest doing the below affirmations while listening to 417 HZ music as it has the power to raise your vibration, balance, and heal you. This frequency helps dissolve feelings of trauma, as well as, any emotional blocks. Some even say it enables you to attract a new life.

860. **I AM** a vortex of forgiveness.

861. **I AM** always releasing pain from the past.

862. **I AM** forgiving, and I live a happy life.

863. **I AM** forgiving myself.

864. **I AM** deserving of love.

865. **I AM** motivated about my new beginning.

866. **I AM** more than enough.

867. **I AM** loved deeply.

868. My wounds are healing, and **I AM** getting stronger every single day.

869. **I AM** trusted.

870. **I AM** connected to this world in a way that matters.

871. I honor the love that we share.

872. **I AM** grateful for the lessons of life.

873. **I AM** excited to love again.

874. **I AM** healing. **I AM** feeling happier with every second of every day.

875. **I AM** filled with inner peace and joy.

876. **I AM** grateful for my past relationship and the lessons that it has taught me.

877. **I AM** healed, and **I AM** ready for a new and fulfilling relationship.

Healing & Clearing

878. I invite joy, peace, and happiness into my heart. I invite light into my life.
879. I attract healthy, loving, and fulfilling relationships.
880. My relationships are a source of joy, love, and happiness.
881. **I AM** loved. **I AM** love. **I AM** in love.
882. The well of unconditional love flows through my heart and heals the past pain.
883. I accept my past with grace, and I let go of it.
884. I forgive myself so that I can forgive others.
885. **I AM** releasing the energies of the past from my mind, body, heart, and energy field. I let the invisible chains fall. **I AM** free to love and trust again.
886. **I AM** confident. I exude self-love, self-respect, and positive self-esteem.
887. **I AM** a whole person. **I AM** an amazing person. **I AM** unique.
888. **I AM** a gift to every person in my life. I beautifully enrich their lives in so many different ways.
889. **I AM** whole, and my heart is full of unconditional love.
890. The love I give to others is coming back to me in so many beautiful ways. My world is full of love.
891. My heart is not broken; my heart is cracked open to more love, light, and joy.

892. **I AM** at peace with my past and everything that happened to me.

893. **I AM** worthy of a loving, devoted, loyal, and committed partner.

894. Every end is also a beginning. I now have an opportunity to manifest and create something really amazing this time.

895. I believe that everything is happening for my higher good.

HEAL ANXIETY

Anxiety is your subconscious fears coming to the surface. Anxiety is always related to your future and concerns that you will not be able to handle something.

Simply put, it is the fear of the unknown and lack of trust in yourself as a co-creator of your life. Anxiety disappears the more you believe you will succeed. Show up as your best self and trust in the Divine to assist you in creating your best life.

Before doing your anti-anxiety affirmations, I would suggest taking deep and mindful breaths for a few moments. It will allow you to expand your consciousness, slow your heartbeat, and open your mind to accepting the suggestions through the affirmations.

896. At this moment, I choose to release the past and look forward to the opportunities that await me.
897. With each new breath, I inhale strength and exhale fear.
898. **I AM** learning that it is safe for me to heal and grow; **I AM** calm.
899. At this moment, I choose to feel calm and peaceful; everything is unfolding as it should.
900. I choose to fill my mind with positive, nurturing, and healing thoughts.

901. There are no mistakes, only lessons to be learned; I always do my best.
902. **I AM** strong, and I can persevere.
903. I approach every situation with openness and confidence.
904. **I AM** in charge of my breathing and choose to slow it down.
905. **I AM** feeling calmer with every given second.
906. **I AM** in control of my emotions; I choose calm and peace.
907. **I AM** cool, calm, and collected.
908. Every breath I inhale calms me, and I let go of my anxiety every breath I exhale.
909. I transcend stress of any kind. I live in peace.
910. **I AM** free of any kind of anxiety or stress.
911. I choose to be stronger than my fears. I choose inner peace.
912. I allow my life to unfold without trying to control it because I know that the Universe has a plan for me, and everything will work out beautifully in my favor.
913. I choose to no longer feed my fears and anxiety; they no longer have control over me.
914. I have an inner well of unconditional love, peace, and wisdom that I tap into whenever I start feeling anxious.

915. I HAVE GOT THIS! I can control what I feel, and I choose serenity and gratitude.
916. I choose my response to challenges. I choose to be calm and peaceful.
917. I embrace my feelings but no longer allow them to control me.
918. **I AM** in control of my emotional state.
919. I inhale love, peace, and light. I exhale my fears and anxieties.
920. **I AM** love, and **I AM** loved. **I AM** safe, and **I AM** protected. The Divine light lives in me.
921. I breathe deeply, and I open my heart widely since there is only love.
922. I no longer fear the future and the unknown because that is where all the potentials and all the possibilities live. I have the power to manifest an amazing future.
923. I let go of my idea about how the present should be; instead, I embrace all the curves and turns of life and expect my miracles.
924. **I AM** an extraordinary being of light and love. **I AM** protected and loved by the Divine.

HEAL DEPRESSION

Depression is the remnants of your past residing in your present. It's the habit of entertaining negative thoughts, worst-case scenarios, and unwillingness to take responsibility for your life. When you are not willing to take responsibility for your life, you fall into the trap of victimhood mentality. In this state, life is no longer happening for you; it's happening to you. You feel you have no energy or strength to fight and survive everything life throws you.

Depression is sometimes a result of unrelenting standards that you place on yourself and a desire to be perfect. Depression can also stem from an incapacity or even unwillingness to see and accept your uniqueness. Depression lifts when you see life as an opportunity and a gift, not a threat.

Remember that nature is always in flow, and it is always in alignment. I invite you to spend a lot of time in nature. Practice these affirmations while you walk in nature, relax by a beach, stare at the beautiful sky, or simply feel the grounding energy of the earth beneath you.

When you inhale, imagine joyful energy entering your body and say affirmations like, "I feel so much gratitude for being alive," or "**I AM** safe, **I AM** calm, **I AM**

Healing & Clearing

loved." When you exhale, imagine exhaling all your negative thoughts, emotions, and fears. See depression as something separate from you but not part of you.

Your soul and spirit can always blossom no matter how wounded your mind might feel. If you take time to consciously connect to your higher self, you will be able to bring that light into your life. Depression is the absence of light, but your higher self can always be allowed to find the light.

925. **I AM** loved, and **I AM** surrounded by people who both love me and like me.
926. **I AM** resilient, and **I AM** a warrior.
927. **I AM** separate from my depression; **I AM** happy and strong.
928. Life is amazing and beautiful; **I AM** grateful for my life.
929. **I AM** in control of my emotions; I choose to be happy.
930. I feel so much gratitude for being alive.
931. **I AM** safe, **I AM** calm, and I choose to be here.
932. I choose to focus on my strengths and improve my weaknesses.
933. I trust my life and know only the best is meant for me.
934. **I AM** in charge of my happiness.
935. **I AM** better than the thoughts that are holding me hostage.

936. **I AM** always accepting of myself.
937. **I AM** freeing myself from my fear and negative thoughts.
938. **I AM** healing every day and continue to heal.
939. I accept myself just the way **I AM**.
940. Love that flows in me is light; from now onwards, I always choose light.
941. **I AM** surrounded by love. **I AM** surrounded by kindness. **I AM** surrounded by light.
942. I cannot change my past, but I have the power to manifest the most compelling future filled with love, light and joy.
943. Every day I feel more and more light entering my life and I welcome it.
944. **I AM** healing, and **I AM** welcoming more and more joy into my life.
945. I have so many things to be grateful for in my life. Thank you, Universe.
946. I celebrate my little victories every day. **I AM** inspired to make my life amazing again.
947. I do the best I can every day.
948. **I AM** so proud of myself and of how far I have come.
949. **I AM** building my world stronger, lighter, and more amazing than it has ever been before. I love watching my transformation.

950. I appreciate what this life has to offer me and I desire to live my life to the fullest.

951. **I AM** loved and appreciated by my friends, family members, and my colleagues. I matter, and my life matters.

HEAL ABANDONMENT

You come into this world alone, and you will leave this world on your own. Yet fear of rejection and the wounds of abandonment are present in so many of our lives. This 3D world creates the illusion of separation of space and time.

Energetically, time does not exist, barriers do not exist, separation does not exist, you are in the Universe, and the Universe is in you. You cannot be abandoned because you are connected to everything. You are ONE with everything. You are part of the Universal Divine Energy.

You may feel that you are not enough for other people. You may try to please them and convince them to love you. By putting others first and prioritizing them, you abandon yourself. You can only be abandoned if you abandon yourself. People come into your life with a reason, a lesson, or a mission. They teach you things, and they help you GROW. They are always aligned with your vibration. Your life is a path you walk, and every person you meet will stay in your experience as long as you are vibrationally aligned.

Many people mistakenly believe that if they were abandoned there is something wrong with them. How about viewing it as the Universe making room for something and somebody better? You deserve the absolute BEST! You deserve a life that is more empowering, more passionate, more loving, more respectful, more committed, and more everything!

Use these affirmations to shift your state from victim to victor. You did not lose people; they lost you!

952. I love and approve of who **I AM** and what **I AM** becoming.
953. I feel the love and vibration of those who always have my back.
954. **I AM** powerful in my own solitude.
955. **I AM** always there for me. Nobody can hurt me unless I allow them to.
956. **I AM** never alone - the whole Universe is in me.
957. **I AM** an incredible gift to the world. I chose only to feel happy thoughts about myself and my life.
958. **I AM** never alone; infinite beings of light surround me.

959. The Universe has made space for new and beautiful people and experiences in my life.

960. I now attract only high-vibrational people into my life.

961. With love and grace, I allow people who do not enhance my life to leave it.

962. I have all the love, happiness, and joy that I need inside of me.

963. I have all the love I need within me. **I AM** enough. Love from the outside is just a bonus.

964. I let go of pain, fears, and doubts. I let go of the hurt. I chose growth.

965. I chose healing, self-love, self-empowerment, and taking my life to soaring heights.

966. **I AM**, and I have always been a whole and beautiful person. I choose to shine bright.

967. I give myself love, care, and attention. I allow myself to feel all the emotions, and I peacefully let go of them. **I AM** free, and **I AM** always loved.

Source Connection

LAW OF ATTRACTION

The Law of Attraction is a sub-law of the Law of Vibration. This is summarized as "You attract what you vibrate." The Universe is impartial, just like your subconscious mind - it does not say this is good, this is bad, this is just, this is unjust, this is fair, this is not fair. Most importantly, it does not understand your preferences. It reads your energy and your vibrations and corresponds to it. If you focus on the things you DO NOT want in your life, you WILL attract them. Where you place your attention is where your energy will flow. This flow can be positive or negative.

When manifesting, it's always a good idea to focus on the inside because that is where your dreams and desires live. If you focus on the outside, you will start feeling 'lack' and let the outside determine the inside.

Start showing up in your life as a co-creator and as a victor. Do not just merely say these affirmations; live them, embody them, and swear by them. If you are new to the world of the Law of Attraction, start by expanding your knowledge about it. Expand your consciousness by becoming an ardent student. Only when you start understanding and practicing different tools do you understand life's "why's," helping you let go of life's "how's."

968. **I AM** a timeless being with co-creative powers with the infinite.

969. I have the power and the ability to create anything I desire.

970. Good things are coming my way.

971. **I AM** always attracting health, vitality, and fun into my life.

972. I attract abundance, wealth, and success into my life effortlessly.

973. **I AM** growing my creative manifestation powers daily.

974. **I AM** positive and passionate.

975. **I AM** absolutely certain of my abilities.

976. **I AM** receiving money into my life just by thinking about it.

977. **I AM** increasingly led to prosperous people who need what I have to offer.

978. **I AM** transforming my entire life using the Law of Attraction Secrets.

979. **I AM** open to all the good God gives me.

980. **I AM** limited by nothing because I have no boundaries.

981. **I AM** certain that my thoughts create my reality, so I focus on the things in my life that I love and enjoy

982. **I AM** always attracting health, vitality, and fun into my life.

983. **I AM** in control of my beliefs, thoughts, desires, and actions.

984. **I AM** an unstoppable force of doing, being, and achieving anything I desire.

985. **I AM** keenly aware that my dreams are turning into reality.

986. God's power is within me. I learn from the past, live in the now, and create my own future.
987. My thoughts are the GPS of my destiny.
988. I manifest my own destiny.
989. **I AM** busting through old tired limiting beliefs. I can do anything.
990. **I AM** co-creator of my reality.
991. I live an incredible life. I manifest the best of everything the world has to offer.
992. **I AM** at peace with where **I AM**, and I have a strong vision for my future.
993. All my needs are taken care of.
994. I visualize and emotionalize my affirmations to activate the Law of Attraction.
995. I manifest everything with confidence and ease.
996. I vibrate happiness, and the Universe sends me more of it.
997. Everything is always working in my favor and my highest good.
998. The Universe always grants all my desires.
999. I always take inspired action.
1000. Every day that passes brings me closer to my dreams and desires.

THE UNIVERSE

You may find yourself wanting to micromanage the Universe. The ego wants to be in control of your manifestation. When you are more connected to your ego than your higher self, you find it hard to trust the Universe. When there is mistrust, letting go is hard. You become attached to the outcome; you create RESISTANCE.

Resistance does not allow for the manifestation to take place. You are stopping your manifestation. If you only knew that the Universe is waiting for you to get out of its way, you would let it do its job. The how and the when is none of your business. Let the Universe deal with that. It knows. Focus on love and happiness. Likes attract likes, be like that which you seek to manifest. The Universe does not speak English or any other language; it speaks vibration. So the happier you are, the more happiness you will attract. The more grateful you are, the more things you will create to be grateful for. Joy attracts more joy.

Use these affirmations when you feel doubts and fears, when you start questioning your manifestations, and you need to strengthen your belief. Everything is possible for the Universe; it is filled with an infinite number of potentials for you to manifest anything.

Source Connection

1001. The Universe wants to give me everything that I desire.
1002. Everything is possible in the Universe; it is filled with an infinite number of possibilities.
1003. I vibrate love, and the Universe sends me my soulmate.
1004. I vibrate happiness, and the Universe sends me more of it.
1005. I trust that the Universe is bringing me the best outcome possible.
1006. I believe that the Universe has an amazing plan for me.
1007. I tap into the infinite resources of the Universe.
1008. **I AM** aligned with Universal Intelligence and abundance.
1009. The Universe is abundant; there is more than enough for everybody.
1010. **I AM** in the Universe, and the Universe is in me. Together we co-create incredible things; together, we create miracles.
1011. I let go, allowing the Universe to summon its unlimited forces and manifest my desire.
1012. No dream or desire is too big for the Universe. Everything is possible for the Universe.
1013. I trust the power of the Universe to heal and to guide me on my path in life.
1014. **I AM** at peace, and all is perfect in the Universe.

MORNING AFFIRMATIONS

You either run the day, or the day runs you. I like reminding people I work with - "the same way you choose your clothes in the morning, the same way you should set an intention for your day." Your morning should not be tainted by the past or yesterday; it should be treated as a blank page. It's your chance to infuse it with the right mental, emotional, and vibrational energy.

If you work out in the morning, you can do your affirmations while you are training. If you do scripting, you can add it to your scripting. If you take time to plan your day, why not write down your intentions as affirmations? Don't be like a cork that is carried aimlessly by the current. Be like a ship that has a destination and a captain.

You can practice your affirmations on your commute to work. You can also start your day with a glass of water infused with the vibration of your affirmations. You will find a further description in the section called "Seven powerful ways to use your affirmations."

1015.   **I AM** filled with the confidence of the morning sun.
1016.   I feel energetic for the day ahead.

Source Connection

1017. **I AM** celebrating each goal that I easily accomplish.

1018. I trust my intuition.

1019. I trust my personal power.

1020. Today **I AM** facing my fears head-on.

1021. **I AM** achieving greatness today.

1022. I acknowledge my own value and self-worth.

1023. **I AM** a powerful co-creator of this day.

1024. I trust my path and my journey.

1025. Today my heart is open to unlimited love.

1026. Today my spirit is open to unlimited wealth.

1027. **I AM** a master manifestor.

1028. Today is full of endless possibilities.

1029. Today and every day, I do my best. I always show up as my best self.

1030. **I AM** celebrating every day of my life because **I AM** life's most precious.

1031. Today and every day, I have the possibility to create incredible things.

1032. **I AM** intentional about my day. Today I choose to be prolific and creative.

1033. I welcome amazing ideas today and every day.

1034. I know it is going to be a great day! Thank you, Universe.

1035. I love the energy of TODAY. I welcome opportunities today and every day.

1036. I expect amazing things to happen to me today.

1037. **I AM** open to blessings of all kinds. Thank you, Universe.

1038. **I AM** consciously creating my day.

> Source Connection

SPIRITUAL

You may often forget that you are so much more than your body. There is so much more to this world and the Universe than you can perceive with your five senses. When you think of yourself in terms of the 3D world and physical reality, you become limited, problems do not have solutions, and miracles do not exist. Yet when you remind yourself that you are ENERGY, that everything is energy, and that you live in a mental Universe, that is when you become unlimited, and everything becomes possible.

You are an extension of the Universe. The Universe is in you, and you are in the Universe. You have the same powers; you are the co-creator.

1039. **I AM** in God, and God is in me.
1040. **I AM** filled with always increasing love for God.
1041. **I AM** connecting with God daily.
1042. **I AM** filled with the Holy Spirit, and the Holy Spirit gives me new life.
1043. **I AM** completely open to God's infinite love.
1044. **I AM** filled with trust and faith in God's divine timing in my life.
1045. **I AM** co-creator with God's infinite power.

1046. **I AM** inspired by the living word of God.

1047. **I AM** guided by God's direction in my life.

1048. **I AM** grateful for everything God has given me and is yet to come.

1049. I believe in God with my whole heart and soul.

1050. I daily call upon the powers of God to renew me.

1051. **I AM** open to God's wisdom.

1052. **I AM** open to God's miracles.

1053. **I AM** open to God's guidance.

1054. My faith in God grows with every breath I take and each new sunrise.

1055. Nothing is impossible with God because with God, all things are possible.

Children

AFFIRMATIONS FOR CHILDREN

It's important to plant the right seeds in children. The earlier you start, the better. At the infant stage, children learn a lot with their mirror neurons that, allow them to learn through imitation. So, if they see you practicing empowering self-talk, and affirmations, they will do it too. Your children will not grow up with limiting beliefs like you might have in your childhood. Your children will grow up to be successful, empowered, and fulfilled individuals.

Your task is always to be mindful of what you tell children. What you tell them, you teach them. Don't invite them to be perfect; invite them to always be and show up as the best version of themselves; whatever their best version on that given day is.

There are two easy ways to practice affirmations for your children. The first would be making them repeat after you when you interact with them. This could be during play, bath time, or eating a meal. The second way to practice affirmations with children is to state these affirmations to them while they are falling asleep. Your encouragement, love, and support will plant the right seeds in their little minds. In fact, later in life, they will constantly hear that they are worthy, they are talented, they are good at something, they are brave, and they are capable of overcoming obstacles.

Children

1056. **I AM** a kind person.
1057. **I AM** happy and grateful for my life.
1058. **I AM** amazing and believe in myself.
1059. **I AM** perfect just the way **I AM**.
1060. **I AM** enough.
1061. **I AM** blessed with confidence and courage.
1062. I can do anything I decide to do.
1063. I accept and love myself.
1064. I deserve to be loved.
1065. I deserve to be happy.
1066. **I AM** open and ready to learn.
1067. It is alright to make errors or mistakes.
1068. I have amazing inner strength.

Gratitude

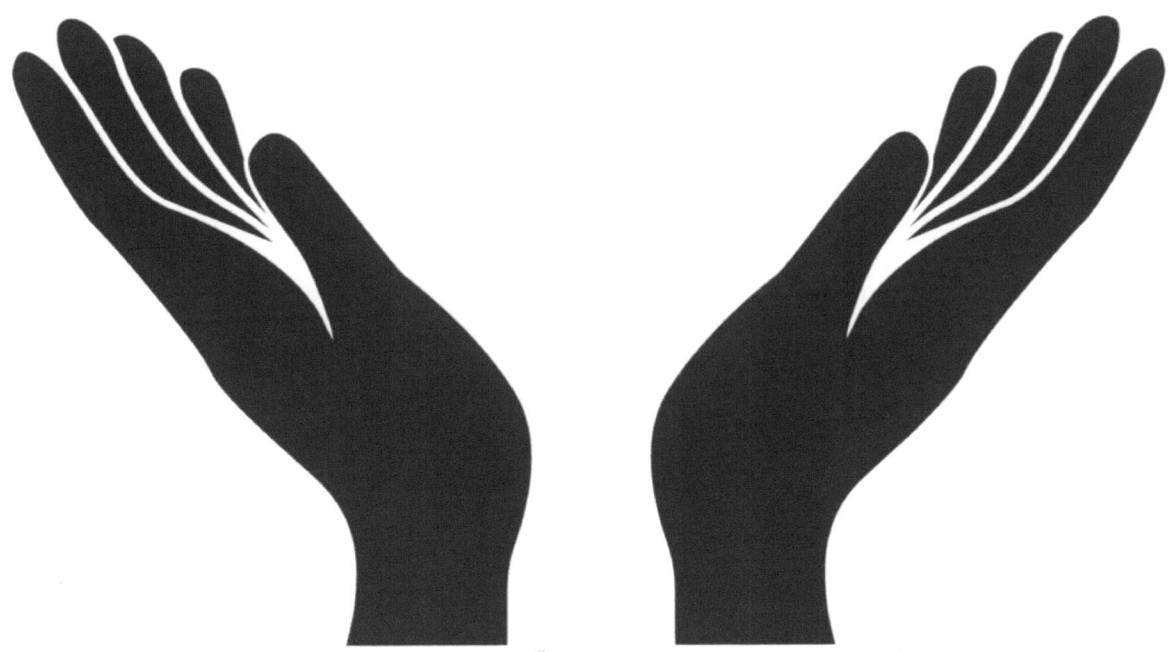

GRATITUDE

Gratitude, even if imaginary, can magically transform your vibration and your energy field. What you appreciate, will appreciate even more. Gratitude takes your attention from what you don't have and places it on everything already present in your life. What you focus on, you invite into your life. Gratitude makes your heart expand. Gratitude makes you feel abundant and prosperous. Gratitude makes you appreciate life and all the amazing, simple things you often take for granted.

Gratitude has the power to ground you in the present moment and shift your vibration when you feel depressed about your past or anxious about your future. Your manifesting journey can sometimes be a rollercoaster of ups and downs. However, gratitude can lessen these extremes. Gratitude will always help you to get into the right vibration when you are feeling sad, down, heartbroken, or at times when you have lost trust in yourself and life.

There are two vibratory states that people manifest from - the state of I need, want, lack, or the state of **I AM**. You can only create and attract things, people, and opportunities from the state of **I AM** co-creator. The **I AM** state naturally flows with gratitude. When you are in a state of gratitude, you are no longer seeking, chasing, and lacking. Gratitude makes your life feel blissful right now. Likes attract likes, so the Law of Attraction gives you more and more things to be grateful for.

What is the best way to practice gratitude affirmations? Always express your gratitude for the Universe when it blesses you with something. It does not matter how small of a thing you are feeling gratitude for: a cup of coffee, a smile from a stranger, someone holding the door for you, a compliment from a stranger, or anything else you experience. Practice appreciating things that you have been taking for granted until now.

Use gratitude for direct manifesting or indirect manifesting. Direct manifesting is where your express your gratitude for events and people from your future in the present tense as if they have already happened. Indirect manifest is being grateful for things that you already have. In this way, with your gratitude vibration, you attract more things to be grateful for.

Here are some examples of gratitude affirmations, "**I AM** grateful for my dream car," "**I AM** so grateful for my loving and respectful partner," "**I AM** beyond grateful for my healing," and "**I AM** grateful for my body's amazing transformation."

If your mission is to attract a miracle, don't make gratitude just something you practice for 5-10 minutes per day. Make gratitude your state of being. Be ALWAYS grateful and watch your life magically transform.

1069. **I AM** grateful for the gift of life.

1070. **I AM** grateful for every morning I open my eyes to a new day.

1071. **I AM** grateful for the opportunity to create the most amazing life I desire to live.

1072. **I AM** grateful to be a co-creator.

1073. **I AM** grateful for all my lessons and the wisdom that they gave me.

1074. **I AM** grateful for the infinite possibilities available to me.

1075. **I AM** grateful for my intuition and inner guidance when choosing things that work in my highest interest.

1076. **I AM** grateful for the inner peace, unconditional love, and universal wisdom that flows through me.

1077. **I AM** grateful for fulfilling and meaningful relationships with my family members, friends, and work colleagues.

1078. **I AM** grateful for the ability to heal and to grow.

1079. **I AM** grateful to my body for its amazing transformation. I love my body.

1080. **I AM** grateful for the beautiful balance I have created in my life.

1081. The more grateful **I AM** the more miracles I attract into my life.

1082. **I AM** grateful for the person **I AM** today, and **I AM** grateful for the person that **I AM** becoming.
1083. **I AM** grateful for all the joy and happiness in my life.
1084. **I AM** grateful for all the love, kindness, and inspiration in my life.
1085. **I AM** grateful for the abundance in all areas of my life.
1086. **I AM** grateful for the ability to live my life with passion, success, and joy.
1087. **I AM** grateful for all the blessings that are coming to my life.
1088. **I AM** grateful for the creativity and inspiration that is flowing to me.
1089. **I AM** grateful for the kindness and love that I receive from others every day.
1090. **I AM** grateful to live an authentic life and to be the best version of myself possible.
1091. **I AM** grateful for my healing. **I AM** grateful for my health.
1092. **I AM** grateful to live an empowered life.
1093. **I AM** grateful to be able to help others.
1094. **I AM** grateful for all my dreams that came true and all those that are about to manifest.
1095. **I AM** grateful for the job I have, and the opportunity to serve others.

1096. **I AM** grateful for my time on this Earth and for being able to do and enjoy all the amazing things this life offers.

1097. **I AM** grateful to be able to leave a legacy.

1098. **I AM** grateful for all the love in my life in all its forms.

1099. **I AM** grateful for the opportunities that every day brings.

1100. **I AM** grateful for all the innate abilities and talents that I have.

1101. **I AM** heartfelt from the beginning of my day to the end.

1102. **I AM** grateful for everything that has brought me to this moment.

1103. **I AM** grateful for the spirit of gratitude.

1104. **I AM** grateful for abundance, prosperity, and the money I receive.

1105. **I AM** grateful for the love in my life, which is ever-flowing and ever-growing.

1106. **I AM** deeply grateful for the wondrous miracles now flowing into my life.

1107. **I AM** grateful for the food I eat and the water that I consume.

1108. **I AM** grateful for my amazing journey.

1109. **I AM** grateful to be able to create so many amazing things.

1110. **I AM** grateful for the guidance and protection of the Infinite Intelligence.

1111. **I AM** grateful for the divine spark in me that allows me to manifest extraordinary things.

SUMMARY

SUMMARY

Words are not mere letters; they are not mere sounds. Words are symbols; they are energy that carry a specific frequency. In the manifesting world, no words are more potent than "**I AM**." It is the beginning and the end of every manifestation. It is the bridge between your dreams and reality. Every word you place after "**I AM**" summons its' existence into reality.

It's easy in society to use words irresponsibly. Watch what you speak to others without thinking. More importantly, watch all the **I AM** self-talk in your head. Self-talk is your repetitive manifesting conversation with the Universe. Use the potential and the power of words in a way that manifest what you desire.

Every time you start your sentence or statement with "**I AM**", you are speaking to yourself. Specifically, you are speaking to the conscious and unconscious parts of yourself. Your subconscious mind does not have eyes. It does not have an analytical mind that would say, "That is valid, that is not; that is true, that is not true; that is good, that is bad," so it BELIEVES anything you say. If you continue repeating it, it becomes a BELIEF that will determine your manifestations.

Your beliefs create your reality. You manifest what you are, not what you want. You are, or you become, what you repeatedly say to yourself. Life does not happen to you; life responds to your thoughts and beliefs. The Universe responds to your vibration. Do an experiment; carry a small notebook, and write down all the negative things you catch yourself saying throughout the day. The next day, do the same, but with positive thoughts and affirmations. Compare the ratio. It will be a true telltale sign of what you are manifesting or what you are not manifesting.

Are there any particular area areas in your life that are not working? Ask yourself, "What beliefs (conscious or less conscious ones) do I have about my relationships, health, money, success, or specific manifestation?" Start reprogramming your mind with the help of the affirmations. You can start changing your life today. You can SPEAK things into existence. Words increase your magnetism and can help you attract anything and everything into your life.

In this book, you will find affirmations for many different areas of your life. Some of them can be combined and used together. Allow your intuition to guide you and select from the numerous affirmations that resonate with you the best. Create your own powerful affirmations in the spare pages. We are all unique, yet in some ways we are all the same. Your heart is a home to beautiful dreams and desires. Each and every one of us has the potential to manifest any desire into reality. It is never too late. You are in the perfect condition to start today.

Always Attracting,

Robert Zink and Agne Lecocq

ASKFIRMATIONS

A belief is a thought that you think over and over again until you start believing it. A belief is merely an assumption, but you hang on to it as if it was real. Many common beliefs include, "Money is hard to make," "I will never be with my partner again," "My partners always cheat on me," "It is not possible to save my business," or "I will never lose weight." Just because you believe something today, doesn't mean it's true forever. However, your belief in a situation makes it easy to manifest. This works with manifesting all your positive and negative beliefs.

Askfirmations are a special type of affirmation that will help you to break the state of your thought process. Whether you are aware or not, you have special behavior and thought patterns. When you break your state using an askfirmation, your mind starts thinking differently. Different thoughts lead to different beliefs, and different beliefs lead to a different reality.

When you are feeling really bad, and stuck in a loop of low-vibration beliefs, doing your regular affirmations might feel like a total lie to your conscious mind. If your conscious mind rejects positive affirmations which it does not believe, there is no chance for the new belief to reach your subconscious mind. This block is because the gap between your current reality, your current feelings, and where you want to be just seems too big. Askfirmations will help you close that gap, therefore shifting your vibration.

ASKFIRMATIONS

So, the next time you catch yourself thinking negative thoughts, take a deep mindful breath, cancel the thought, and replace it with an askfirmation. An askfirmation is a statement in the form of a question that works to get the mind to imagine a positive situation. Askfirmations usually start with the phrases "What if," "Wouldn't it be nice," and "Why." These three phrases are vibrational keys to unlock a new way of thinking.

Turning the regular affirmation, "**I AM** manifesting a miracle," into an askfirmation might look like this, "What if my miracle has already manifested?", "Wouldn't it be nice to feel the blessing of my miracle manifested," or "Why is the Universe allowing me to manifest so many miracles." These askfirmations allow your mind to feel as if the desire has already manifested.

Here are a few more examples of askfirmations. "What if my partner is deeply in love with me?" "What if tomorrow, my life is taking an amazing turn?" "What if everything **I AM** going through is bringing me closer to my dreams and desires?" "What if **I AM** already healed?" "Wouldn't it be nice if my partner called me?" "Wouldn't it be nice if my interview went well?" "Wouldn't it be nice if they hired me?" "Why does my specific person desire me so much?" "Why am I attracting all these amazing opportunities?" "Why is it so easy to manifest big amounts of money?" "Why is it so easy to lose weight?"

Try putting your affirmations in the form of askfirmations and see what happens. Do you feel your manifestation is closer when you use askfirmations? Is an askfirmations easier for you to believe? If askfirmations excite your energy field, create positive vibrations, and shift your beliefs, use them regularly to speed up your manifestation.

NOTES

NOTES

www.ingramcontent.com/pod-product-compliance
Lightning Source LLC
Chambersburg PA
CBHW041627170426
43195CB00034B/44